BIOETHICS

THE BASICS

Exploring some of the most controversial yet important questions facing us today, *Bioethics: The Basics* is an engaging introduction to the study of Bioethics.

It gradually introduces readers to the foundational principles, theories and issues which form the core of biomedical and health care ethics exploring such questions as:

- Can ethics keep pace with modern technology?
- How can we ensure that scientific research is for everyone's benefit?
- Why do medicine and health care require a high standard of ethics?
- What theories help health care professionals make difficult ethical decisions?
- Who should decide what is in a patient's best interests?
- Can we achieve justice in health care?

With real world examples, suggestions for further reading and a comprehensive glossary, this is an authoritative introduction for anyone interested in the study of bioethics.

Alastair V. Campbell is Chen Su Lan Centennial Professor and Director of the Centre for Biomedical Ethics at the National University of Singapore. He is founding editor of the *Journal of Medical Ethics* and a past President of the International Association of Bioethics as well as the author of ten books and numerous articles in the field. He is also an elected Fellow of The Hastings Center, New York, an Honorary Vice-President of the Institute of Medical Ethics, UK and a Corresponding Fellow of the Royal Society of Edinburgh.

The Basics

BIOETHICS

THE BASICS

Alastair V. Campbell

Routledge
Taylor & Francis Group

LONDON AND NEW YORK

First published 2013
by Routledge
2 Park Square, Milton Park, Abingdon, Oxon OX14 4RN

Simultaneously published in the USA and Canada
by Routledge
711 Third Avenue, New York, NY 10017

Routledge is an imprint of the Taylor & Francis Group, an informa business

British Library Cataloguing in Publication Data
A catalogue record for this book is available from the British Library

Library of Congress Cataloging in Publication Data
Campbell, Alastair V.
Bioethics: the basics / Alastair V. Campbell.
pages cm – (The basics)
1. Medical ethics. 2. Bioethics. 3. Social medicine. I. Title.
R724.C3257 2013
174.2–dc23   2013005003

ISBN: 978-0-415-50409-6 (hbk)
ISBN: 978-0-415-50408-9 (pbk)
ISBN: 978-0-203-70396-0 (ebk)

Typeset in Bembo
by Taylor & Francis Books

CONTENTS

PREFACE

Writing a book about 'the basics' of your academic discipline is both challenging and refreshing. The challenge is to describe the complexities of the subject in an accessible style, yet without distorting or simplifying the issues. It's a challenge which every 'ivory tower' academic should surely attempt at least once in a lifetime. At the same time, it is a refreshing experience and (most of the time) I have enjoyed it. To be able to write without constant referencing and without forever worrying about the kind of nit-picking criticisms which academic reviewers are likely to offer gives a feeling of freedom to write more spontaneously and informally. This is meant to be a book that speaks directly to non-experts in the field, especially to those who are facing the kind of ethical problems I describe. If the book makes sense to that readership, I will be very happy indeed!

I have had help from several colleagues in this task, some assisting with literature searches and others giving detailed commentary on some of the chapters, especially ones where I felt out of my depth. I was especially helped by those who guided me in summarising several religious and cultural approaches outside my own tradition for the chapter on perspectives on bioethics. Thanks for this are due to Alireza Bagheri, Nancy Berlinger, Subrata Chattopadhyay, Soraj Hongladarom, Paul Ulhas Macneill and Voo Teck Chuan (but of course any remaining errors are entirely mine). Donald Hill gave great help with very focused comments on the style and the philosophical aspects of the book, and Gerard Porter on the ethics of international research. Lisbeth Nielsen and Leo de Castro helped me find sources on research ethics and research integrity, and Jacqueline Chin to chart my way through the feminist literature.

Special thanks are due to Syahirah A. Karim, a Research Associate at my Centre. She has tirelessly (and always cheerfully) worked both on research for the book and on getting the chapters into a publishable form. Without her consistent and skilled help, this book would never have been completed.

Finally, writing this work has been a family affair – with one son a philosopher, another a paramedic and my wife a lawyer, I have never been short of support and understanding, including help with cases and relevant literature. It has all helped to make this a truly rewarding experience.

Alastair V. Campbell
Centre for Biomedical Ethics,
National University of Singapore
September 2012

ABBREVIATIONS

ART	assisted reproductive technology
CH	capability to be healthy
ELSI	ethical, legal and social implications
ESCs	embryonic stem cells
IAB	International Association of Bioethics
iPSCs	induced pluripotent stem cells
IVF	*in vitro* fertilization
NIH	National Institutes of Health
PVS	persistent vegetative state
VE	virtue ethics
WHO	World Health Organization
WMA	World Medical Association

WHAT IS BIOETHICS?

WHAT IS BIOETHICS?

Is health care just a business like any other, or should health care professionals have a higher standard of ethics? Should we invent a pill that enables people to live for hundreds of years? Have parents the right to use science to design the kind of children they want? Does everyone have an equal right to health care, whatever it costs? Is abortion the same as killing babies? Should we create creatures that are partly animal and partly human? Is it OK to sell our body parts, such as one of our kidneys, like we buy and sell our material possessions, our cars or our mobile phones? Should the state force people to adopt healthy life styles? Should mercy killing be made legal? Does it matter if our current use of natural resources is likely to totally destroy the environment in a few years from now?

These are the kinds of questions raised and discussed by bioethics. As we shall see, the subject began with concerns about the morality of doctors and other health care workers, but as science and technology have opened up a myriad of possibilities for changing human life, it has broadened out to include a wide range of ethical issues related to human health and welfare. Although, literally, the word 'bioethics' just means the 'ethics of life', I shall restrict its meaning to those areas of human life in which medicine and the biomedical sciences can affect human well-being – for good or for ill.

HISTORY

In some respects bioethics has a very long history. Concerns about how doctors treat their patients go back to ancient times, with ethical codes like the Hippocratic Oath and the Charaka Samhita Oath of Initiation setting ethical norms; and in the nineteenth and early twentieth centuries the rapid expansion of the biological sciences began to raise new questions about the possibilities for human progress and the potential conflicts between science and religion. But the birth and rapid development of modern bioethics came as a result of the atrocities of the Second World War.

HUMAN GUINEA PIGS

We can begin with the Nazi War Crime Tribunals held in Nuremberg from 1945 to 1949 in the aftermath of the Second World War. These trials revealed a grisly catalogue of crimes against humanity, many of them perpetrated by doctors and involving ruthless and lethal experimentation on the inmates of concentration camps. (Many years later it was to emerge that equally horrifying experiments were carried out on Chinese prisoners by Japanese doctors (Nie et al., 2008), but these were hushed up by the American government in a deal that allowed it access to the results (Harris, 1994).) Out of the horror of the Nuremberg trials came the first stages of the growth of bioethics. The Nuremberg Code of 1947 (Office of History 1947) laid down fundamental principles for the protection of the subjects of medical experiments, most notably stressing the necessity for fully informed and voluntary consent. Around the same time, the World Medical Association was founded and it produced the Geneva Code of Medical Ethics, an updated version of the ancient Hippocratic Oath. (Texts of these and other documents can be found in the Appendix.) The Code required that 'The health of my patient must be my first consideration'.

Thus modern bioethics comes in part from medical ethics and specifically from the ethics of medical research. Awareness had grown that doctors cannot always be trusted to act ethically and that the traditional reliance on professional self-governance was simply not enough. The somewhat smug traditional approach to the nobility of the medical profession is well captured in these comments by a long-serving chairman of the British Medical Association Ethics Committee:

> In the relations of the practitioner to his fellows, while certain established customs and even rules are written and must be written, the principal influence to be cultivated is that of good fellowship. Most men know what is meant by 'cricket' and the spirit of the game. Difficulties and differences will arise, but most of them can be successfully met by mutual goodwill and recognition of the other fellow's point of view.
>
> (British Medical Association, 1974)

The idea that somehow the rules of cricket sum up morality must surely have been shaken by the revelation of medical involvement in acts of gross inhumanity during the war. Yet, in the decade and a half following Nuremberg, a sense of complacency seems to have remained in the medical profession. The atrocities committed in the war were seen as the aberration of a few psychopathic individuals driven by an evil ideology, but the profession as whole could still be seen as noble and trustworthy.

This illusion could not last. It began to crumble when writers on both sides of the Atlantic revealed what was happening in the ever-burgeoning area of medical research and drug trials. The most notorious of these unethical research trials was the US federally funded Tuskegee Syphilis Study, which lasted from 1932 to 1972. In this study, 399 impoverished African American men in the tertiary stages of syphilis were enrolled for observation of the final phases of the disease when left untreated (Jones, 1993). At the time, syphilitic patients were known to suffer significantly higher rates of mortality and **morbidity**, typically relating to cardiovascular and central nervous system pathologies. However, subjects were not told of their diagnosis, nor were they given access to effective medication (penicillin) once it became available in the 1940s. The study was finally disbanded only after a media exposé. This shocking episode in the history of American medicine was finally the subject of an apology by the President of the United States in 1997, 25 years after it ended. Yet even as this apology was being made, more evidence of similarly outrageous research was emerging. From 1946 to 1948, the US Public Health Service and the Pan American Sanitary Bureau worked with several Guatemalan government agencies to do medical research – paid for by the US government – that involved deliberately exposing people to sexually transmitted diseases. The researchers apparently were trying to see if penicillin, then relatively new, could prevent infections in the 1,300 people exposed to syphilis, gonorrhoea or chancroid. Those infected with syphilis included soldiers, prostitutes, prisoners and mental patients.

Back in the late 1960s these shocking examples were still not generally known about, but enough was revealed by the writings of H. K. Beecher in the USA (*Research and the Individual*, 1970) and M. H. Pappworth in the UK (*Human Guinea Pigs*, 1967) to make the international medical community realize that all was not well with medical research. Already in 1964 the World Medical Association (WMA) had published the first version of the Declaration of Helsinki, setting down rules for the ethical conduct of medical research. The debate about how to monitor and control medical research to make sure it stays within ethical bounds has continued ever since. Over the years the Declaration has gone through six revisions, with the latest version adopted in October 2008 at the WMA's General Assembly (see Appendix).

MEDICAL MAGIC

However, dubious research practice was not the only reason for the burgeoning of bioethics in the decades following the Second World War. An even more potent influence came from the dramatic expansion of medicine's capacity to save lives and either cure or prevent disease, through the production of a vast range of pharmaceuticals and vaccines, the refinement of life-saving medical technologies such as dialysis and heart-lung machines, and major improvements in surgical techniques. In those heady days it must have seemed to many people that the conquest of disease and disability was just around the corner. Yet, of course, every new advance brought fresh ethical problems. With the advent of organ transplantation, it became necessary to find a new definition of death – '**brain death**' – so that the organs to be transplanted would remain viable; and the ability to keep people alive on machines did not necessarily mean that the *quality* of a patient's life was improved or even maintained. Moreover, the massive commercial power of the transnational pharmaceutical and medical technology industries could also pose a major threat to health, through the medicalization of all human experience from birth to death, as Ivan Illich argued in his controversial book, *Medical Nemesis* (1974).

NEW COLLABORATIONS

I shall be discussing some of these new ethical challenges later, but for the moment we can see how the idea that doctors alone could discuss and settle these new ethical challenges became quite unsustainable. These were issues of intimate concern to patients and of vital interest to society as a whole. The radical changes in medicine demanded a move to a more open, nuanced and multi-disciplinary medical ethic, and one that opened the decisions of the profession to public debate. As a result, new institutions and new academic journals were founded in both the UK and the USA. In 1967 The Hastings Center, an independent non-partisan institute for the study of ethics in the life sciences, was set up in New York State, and it commenced publication of the *Hastings Center Report* four years later. Around the same time, the Society for the Study of Medical Ethics emerged in Britain as a result of a medical student initiative to get medical ethics discussed in medical schools; and in 1975 the Society joined forces with the *British Medical Journal* to produce the *Journal of Medical Ethics*. From the start, these new institutions represented an active collaboration between doctors and other health professionals, philosophers, theologians, lawyers and social scientists. Medical ethics was breaking away from its origins in the closed professional circle of doctors and coming of age as an independent and critical scrutiny of the ethical issues emerging in medicine and in health care as a whole.

Since those early days of bioethics there has been a vast expansion of centres and institutes devoted to bioethics and of journals in the field, as well as an increasing presence of medical ethics in the core curricula of medical schools. But, since it is not the purpose of this book to give a full history of the discipline, I will merely pick out three main developments that have had a profound effect on the increasing complexity of bioethics.

HEALTH AS A PUBLIC GOOD

The first of these is the influence of the World Health Organization (WHO). The WHO was founded in 1948 as a specialized agency of the United Nations. Early in its history it supported a wide definition of health as 'complete physical, mental and social well-being, not merely negatively as the absence of disease or infirmity'. (World Health Organization, 1948) In line with this broad approach, the WHO has been very active in issues of global public health, dealing with such issues as breast feeding, tobacco use, HIV/AIDS and global **pandemics**. The WHO approach focuses on justice in health care resources, as well as a recognition of the social determinants of ill-health – poverty, unemployment, lack of education and absence of adequate food, clean water and sanitation. These themes have entered into bioethical discussion, albeit some-what tardily, and the subset of bioethics which deals with issues of justice has grown ever more important. This represents a departure from an exclusive focus on the practitioner–patient relationship to a critical study of why people suffer ill-health and how the social and political factors creating it should be tackled. More recently still, environmental ethics has come into the field, provoked parti-cularly by global warming and its detrimental effects on human health. These issues will be discussed in the last chapter of this book, entitled 'Justice'.

THE GENOME REVOLUTION

A second major influence on contemporary bioethics has been the exponential development of human genetics following the mapping of the **human genome**. This has raised some key questions about the determinants of human behaviour, the potential for predicting disease and disability and the protection of human privacy. No other field of bioethics has had such a concentration of scholarship, partly because of a decision of the funders of the human genome mapping project to devote 5 per cent of the funds to the ethical, legal and social implications (ELSI) of the scientific discoveries. The issues uncovered by all this investment of effort will be discussed later (in Chapter 5), but for the moment we can note that this has led to a broadening out of bioethics from a focus on health care and the clinical relationship to 'biomedical ethics', the study of the ethical implications of findings in the biosciences, particularly in genetics.

GLOBALIZATION

Finally, the founding of the International Association of Bioethics (IAB) in Amsterdam in 1994 marks a significant new feature of bioethics, its emergence from a European–American domination to an attempt to be truly global and multicultural. The origin of the Association is significant in itself. Its first President, Peter Singer, had been subject to a form of censorship of his views on such controversial topics as euthanasia, by mass disruptions of meetings in Europe at which he was the main speaker. The founders of the Association saw this as a symptom of a widespread attempt to stifle free debate in bioethics in a range of countries where religious beliefs or other ideologies claimed a normative position. The constitution of the IAB states the objectives of the Association to be:

1   To facilitate contacts and the exchange of information between those working in bioethics in different parts of the world;
2   To organize and promote periodic international conferences in bioethics;
3   To encourage the development of research and teaching in bioethics;
4   To uphold the value of free, open and reasoned discussion of issues in bioethics.

In addition, the IAB constitution is designed to prevent national or cultural imperialism by requiring that the 21-member Board of the Association be drawn from all regions of the world and that no one country can have more than three members on the Board. The opportunity is thus created for a genuine dialogue at an international level, encouraging a diversity of approaches to bioethics.

BIOETHICS COMES OF AGE

In summary, then, bioethics has 'come of age' over the past few decades. Beginning from a critical appraisal of traditional approaches to medical ethics in the practitioner–patient relationship, bioethics has broadened its horizons to include the life sciences more generally, the social and political dimensions of health care and the challenges of globalization and multiculturalism. Matching this expansion has been a flowering of different ways of tackling the questions raised and an awareness that, as science and technology continue to throw up new possibilities, the ethical questions will become ever more complex. Whatever else might be said, it is clear that bioethics is not going to get easy answers to all the questions it raises!

WHAT ABOUT THE LAW?

I have been stressing the complexity of bioethics and the difficulty of finding simple answers to the dilemmas we face, but an obvious question now arises – can't these problems and dilemmas best be solved by improving existing laws and drawing up new ones, if required? Why bother with ethical debate, if legislation can provide the answers?

Clearly, there are examples of how reforming the law can help with some issues. For example, abuses in medical experimentation can be prevented to some degree by a detailed set of regulations (as is the case with the Federal Regulations in the USA). Another area might be laws governing new birth technologies, of which a well-known example is the UK Human Fertilization and Embryology Act (2008) (United Kingdom, 2008). Laws preventing the use of genetic information to discriminate against people in health insurance or employment have also been passed in some US states (Department of Labor et al.). And a few countries or states have enacted provisions to allow doctors to end or assist in ending the lives of people at their request (often called 'death with dignity' legislation) (Focarelli, 2009).

But already the problems with using the law to solve the problems of bioethics begin to be obvious. In the first place, there is widespread disagreement about some of the issues mentioned above.

Examples would be the use of human embryos in research, which is permitted in the UK and some other countries but banned by the law in others; and euthanasia, which is permitted by the law in some places, but is a criminal offence in others. Moreover, many countries lack any kind of legislation on some areas, which are controlled by law in other countries. The result is '**medical tourism**'. For example, infertile couples may travel to a country which permits commercial **surrogacy** if they are prevented from arranging this in their own country.

So, in controversial areas of bioethics, the law provides no consistent international answers. There have, however, been some attempts to reach international agreements in bioethics. The main proponent of this has been UNESCO, another agency of the United Nations. In October 2005 its General Council adopted the *Universal Declaration on Bioethics and Human Rights*. The first aim of the Declaration is stated as follows:

> ... to provide a universal framework of principles and procedures to guide States in the formulation of their legislation, policies or other instruments in the field of bioethics.
>
> (United Nations Educational Scientific and Cultural Organization 2005, Article 2(a))

As is clear from this phrasing, this Declaration is merely advisory. It cannot determine what actual laws or policies are adopted by member states. Moreover, the vagueness and generality of its statements have been criticized by a number of writers – yet only such broad phrasing was likely to have any chance of international agreement.

It seems, then, that looking for a solution in universally accepted laws is a bit of a wild goose chase. However, this does not mean that the law is of no use or relevance in bioethics. But, instead of imagining that it can provide universally applicable, clear-cut answers, we can look for its help in two respects. First, the law defines limits to the permissible actions of doctors and others involved in science or in health care. These limits may be quite broad, but they are important nonetheless. The requirement to gain fully informed consent is one good example of a legal limit of this kind. This clearly establishes that treatment of, or experimentation on, people who are able to make their own decisions is a form of assault, if done without their consent (unless there are special circumstances – such as a medical emergency – which justify not getting consent). A second example is medical confidentiality, which provides the secure conditions under which people can share intimate details of their lives for the sake of effective treatment. Third, the absolute prohibition of fraud or deception in research prevents the abuse of the power which the special knowledge possessed by doctors or scientists gives them. These three central pillars of professional and scientific integrity are almost universally backed up by laws governing professional practice throughout the world.

A second way in which the law is relevant to bioethics is in the detailed judgments of courts, the elaboration of case law. There are many landmark cases, in which legal analysis has helped to clarify the ethical principles at stake and to offer judgments, which provide precedents for future similar cases. Notable examples are judgments about the adequacy of consent to medical treatment, discontinuation of tube feeding of patients in persistent vegetative state (PVS), switching off life support at the patient's request, non-treatment of severely disabled newborns, and separation of **conjoined twins** when this will lead to the death of one of them. In all these cases, judges have explored in detail the underlying ethical principles and the relationship of these principles to fundamental legal doctrines. Thus medical law, while not to be confused with bioethics, is clearly a valuable ally in the quest to get to comprehensive and well-argued solutions to the problems created by advances in science and technology as they affect human health.

METHODS

If the law does not provide the whole answer, how, then, is bioethics to proceed? What methods can it use to tackle the questions it raises?

GETTING THE FACTS RIGHT

We have already seen that the subject is essentially multidisciplinary, so we can expect a variety of methods to be used. A basic requirement is that we get our facts right, since we cannot base valid ethical judgments on inaccurate or inadequate information. That is why medical and scientific experts are essential to the discipline. For example, there has been a major international controversy recently over the use of human embryos to derive **embryonic stem cells** (ESCs) for research and possible treatments. Some opponents of the use of ESCs have argued that there is now no need for such cells, since **induced pluripotent stem cells** (iPSCs), which can be derived from adults without causing them harm, can be used in exactly the same way. But is this claim correct? Only a scientific expert in the field can answer this factual question. Another example would be claims that patients diagnosed with PVS can in fact recover consciousness and communication (Lotze et al., 2011, Estraneo et al., 2010), but others have argued that these cases of recovery are because the diagnosis was not correctly made in the first place. Again, only expert opinion can provide an answer to this disagreement. Thus bioethics requires the highest standard of medical and scientific information (and this needs to be constantly updated), otherwise its conclusions about the ethical issues are worthless. It is also essential to be clear about those areas in which there is still scientific uncertainty, with more than one conclusion a possibility at this stage. The arguments become dishonest when such uncertainty is denied and proponents present only those conclusions favourable to their moral viewpoint (something which has often occurred in the stem cell debate).

CLINICAL WISDOM

A second area of needed expertise is what can be loosely termed 'clinical wisdom'. This is a difficult concept and could easily be misunderstood. We have already seen how bioethics has broken free from the 'doctors know best' mentality, which saw the views of patients or of the general public as too biased or ill-informed to be of relevance to the decisions doctors were making. But the pendulum can swing too far the other way. The clinical encounter is not a straightforward provider–consumer relationship, on a par with, say, the marketing of TV sets or second-hand cars. In those encounters 'the customer is king', and it is up to the purchaser to make choices that suit his or her preferences, including such factors as quality and price. In such business transactions the Latin saying *caveat emptor* ('let the buyer beware') applies. In other words it is up to the customer to look after his or her own interests and to spot dodgy deals.

But, despite attempts to model health care on this kind of market transaction, the reality of the clinical relationship is very different. In most medical encounters we are no ordinary 'consumers'. Fear of illness, perhaps of imminent death, makes most of us vulnerable and uncertain. We look to health professionals for information and advice, but also for support and understanding – not something we would expect from a used-car salesman! For this reason, some writers have described the relationship as 'covenantal' rather than 'contractual' (May, 1975), by which is meant that the professional offers a commitment to the welfare of the patient, which cannot be simply specified as a list of deliverables. For, in addition to the exchange of goods and services for a fee, there is the forging of a therapeutic relationship, and this in itself can affect the recovery of the patient. (These aspects of the professional relationship are discussed more fully in Chapter 4.) We can now see why bioethics needs not only the expertise of biomedical scientists: it also requires the insights of clinicians who know the personal cost, to patients – but also to practitioners – of a daily encounter with our vulnerability as human beings.

SOCIAL SCIENCE PERSPECTIVES

However, clinical wisdom, though important, is not enough to gain an adequate perspective on bioethics. When we are in the midst of things, we can lack the critical judgement to see the numerous factors that affect the way problems are encountered and solutions are sought. Here a different expertise is needed, that of the social sciences. This group of disciplines can be applied to bioethics in various ways. The tools of political science can be used to study how health care systems and other scientific enterprises function, identifying the factors that can influence ethical decisions and policies. (In Chapter 5 we shall see examples of this in the 'tissue economy' that have affected the way the procurement of human organs and tissue has been skewed by economic factors.) Social scientists can also look critically at the way professions operate in society – Eliot Freidson's devastating critique of American medicine, *Profession of Medicine* (1988), provides a famous example. In this book he argued that the claim to be ethical and trustworthy was merely a device for securing wealth and social prestige, not in any sense a genuine ethical commitment. Social scientific research methods, such as surveys, interviews and focus groups, can also be used to establish the opinions, beliefs and practices of doctors, scientists, patients and the general public. This can often yield surprising results, for example, that cancer patients consistently rate their quality of life higher than do those caring for them (Papadopoulos et al., 2011, Mellon et al., 2006). Such insights can help health providers to formulate a more sensitive and helpful approach to communicating with these patients.

PHILOSOPHICAL CRITIQUE

But, while all of these methods provide valuable information and insights, we do not yet seem to be at the heart of bioethics. That is because finding out what *is* the case does not tell us what *ought to be* the case. To take an extreme example: if surveys revealed that a majority in our society believed that there should be a policy of sterilizing all persons with an IQ of less than 90, to reduce the 'burden' on society by preventing them from producing 'deficient' offspring, this fact would not establish that the policy would be ethically right. To put it simply: 'is' and 'ought' convey two quite different types of claim – one is purely descriptive ('most people favour compulsory sterilization'), but the other is evaluative ('forcibly sterilizing people is wrong'). History is littered with examples of commonly held views which we would now regard as morally wrong; for example, that women should not be allowed to vote or receive higher education, or that some races are morally inferior to others.

Thus the main method of bioethics has to be concerned with the *justification* of moral views, not just with a description of who thinks what, or of the social factors that influence people's views. That is why the whole of the next chapter will be devoted to explaining and assessing a range of moral theories, all of which attempt to show how moral claims are justified. The discipline that formulates such theories is usually called 'moral philosophy', or sometimes (confusingly), 'ethics'. The latter name is confusing because it can be used in so many different ways, as can the words, 'morals' or 'morality'. These terms can describe a range of things – personal moral views, professional codes of conduct, the beliefs and attitudes of social groups ('young people today have no morals') or of whole societies ('our country has lost its ethical bearings') and, finally, 'ethics' can be used to describe the critical study of morality. To avoid this confusion, we need to describe the method of assessing different ways of justifying moral views as 'philosophical ethics' or, more simply, as 'moral philosophy', since the discipline of philosophy is all about assessing the validity of claims, whether these be to truth, beauty or goodness.

APPLICATIONS

However, this important point about the critical function of bioethics should not blind us to the fact that it also has important practical applications. It is not merely an academic exercise, of interest only to scholars who enjoy debating theoretical issues. There are many ways in which bioethics has been, and can be, applied to practical issues. The first is the influence it has had on professional education. This has been true not only of medical education, where courses in critical medical ethics are becoming a standard part of the medical curriculum worldwide. It is also a key component in health professional education generally. It was an early feature of nursing education, and the nursing associations have been as active as the medical ones in formulating and revising ethical codes. The other professions related to medicine have followed suit, with courses in ethics for dentists, pharmacists, physiotherapists and paramedics taking a central place in preparation for practice. The important factor here is that these courses have become not just rote learning of an ethical code, but critical reflections on practice, using case studies to ground the discussion in clinical reality.

A second area of practical application has been the setting up of national bioethics advisory bodies in many countries, some sponsored by government agencies and others funded independently of government. (Examples of the former are the Presidential Commission for the Study of Bioethical Issues in the USA, and of the latter, the Nuffield Council on Bioethics in the UK.) These bodies are usually multidisciplinary and multi-professional, and they can have a major influence on government policies and on legislation, especially in newly emerging areas, like stem cell research and therapy.

A third aspect of modern bioethics is its participation in biomedical research through the study of the ELSI aspects of scientific studies, and also through independent scholarly research of key issues in bioethics. There is now a wealth of scholarly literature in the field and a large number of academic journals, with major sponsorship of the research coming from the European Commission, the National Institutes of Health (NIH) in the USA and the Wellcome Trust in the UK, as well as funding from many countries across the globe.

Finally, the study of bioethical issues is rapidly becoming an important feature of high school education, not only in courses in the biological sciences, but also more widely in courses on values and citizenship. This promises well, not only for the burgeoning of scholarship in bioethics, but also for a better-informed public who can take a more knowledgeable and active part in future debates about the new policies and improved legislation which many of the emerging issues in the field will require. Eventually, bioethics must not be seen as an area restricted to academics and professionals. The ethical issues which bioethics explores affect us all.

HOW TO USE THIS BOOK

The plan of the following chapters is as follows: Chapters 2 and 3 examine in detail the theoretical background of the subject, first by describing a range of moral theories and then by looking at other perspectives on bioethics, including the approaches of five major world religions; the last three chapters turn to practical applications, with Chapter 4 dealing with clinical ethics, Chapter 5 with research ethics and research integrity, and Chapter 6 with justice in public health, health care delivery and global health.

You should feel free to dip into the text at different places according to your interests. You will find a detailed list of contents and an index to help you find the relevant parts to read. There is no need to read the theoretical chapters first, though they may help you to gain a richer understanding of the ethical issues, either before or after you read about some of the practical issues. Finally, I have given suggestions for further reading and other resources at the end of each chapter, so that you can follow up on topics of special interest to you, and a short glossary is provided to help you understand some of the more technical terms used (but I have tried to avoid these as much as possible). You will find the first instance of any glossary entry highlighted in bold. I hope you enjoy reading this book as much as I have enjoyed writing it!

RESOURCES AND FURTHER READING

Both Cambridge and Oxford University presses have published readers in bioethics – *The Cambridge Textbook of Bioethics*, edited by Peter A. Singer and A. M. Viens (2008); and *Bioethics* (in the Oxford Readings in Philosophy series), edited by John Harris (2001). These contain between them a good range of scholarly articles covering most of the areas discussed in this book. If you are interested in the history of the subject you should consult the volume by Henk ten Have and Bert Gordijn (2001) for European developments, and the account by Albert Jonsen (2003) of the 'birth of bioethics' in the USA. But these books are limited to developments in the West. To get the global picture, consult *Bioethics around the Globe*, edited by Catherine Myser (2011). This contains some hard-hitting essays revealing the cultural biases in the subject area. For a different take on bioethics, relating it to environmental issues and to broader scientific concerns such as genetic modification of crops, see *Bioethics: An Introduction for the Biosciences*, by Ben Mepham (2008).

The best way to discover the latest discussions in the field is to consult journals and the Internet. For a list of journals and many other resources see either http://bioethics.georgetown.edu/ publications/scopenotes/sn38.htm, a website run by Georgetown University, or the NIH website, http://bioethics.od.nih.gov/. For details on medical malpractice, see http://www.loc.gov/law/help/ medical-malpractice-liability/index.php. There are many journals in the field, of variable quality, so you should start first with the *Journal of Medical Ethics*, or *Bioethics*, or *the Hastings Center Report*. For medical law, there is again a wide range of journals. You could start by consulting *Medical Law Review* or the *Journal of Law, Medicine, and Ethics*. There are also many blogs, giving you the up-to-date news, recent journal articles and (quite often) scandals. Among the liveliest and (probably) most reliable ones are: http://blog. practicalethics.ox.ac.uk/ and http://www.thehastingscenter.org/ BioethicsForum/Default.aspx, but you could also consult http:// www.medpedia.com/news_analysis/56-Bioethics-Discussion-Blog.

In later chapters I shall be suggesting other resources, related to the specific topics discussed there.

MORAL THEORIES

INTRODUCTION

In the last chapter we saw how the task of working out what we *ought* to do in face of the numerous dilemmas in bioethics seems to lie at least partly with moral philosophy in its specification of moral theories. Now we must look at the range of these theories and try to see how adequate they are to this task. To bring the various theories to life, I want you to imagine yourself faced with a moral dilemma, a situation in which you have to make a very difficult moral choice and it is hard to know which 'horn' of the dilemma is the better one to opt for. The situation I describe is imaginary, but it is based on the kind of actual choices which some people have had to face, especially in situations of war or other violent conflicts. I am using this imaginary scenario, rather than an actual case drawn from bioethics, so that we can see the general features of moral theories before discussing how they might apply in medicine and science.

THE MAYOR'S DILEMMA

You are the elected mayor of a small village on an island which has been occupied by a foreign power as part of the war it is waging against your country. A colonel of the occupying army has been sent to the island to deal with a group of three resistance fighters who have killed four of his soldiers. He has taken 80 hostages from among the villagers and has had them marched into the village square. Two of the captured guerrillas are already in the square under armed guard. The third guerrilla, and two girls from the village who had helped him hide, have already been tortured and executed. Their grossly mutilated bodies are in full view of all the hostages. The colonel hands you a machine gun (which turns out to be unloaded) and orders you to beat the two surviving captives to death in front of the villagers. If you do this at once, the colonel says he will spare the lives of the 80 hostages (sending them instead to a labour camp), but, if you refuse, then you and all 80 hostages will be instantly mowed down by his soldiers' machine guns. You must decide in the next few minutes. What will you do? And why is it the right thing to do?

Before thinking what you would do, you should realize that in such situations you cannot be sure what will happen next. If the guerrillas are killed by you, the colonel may order his soldiers to shoot the hostages anyway, 'to teach them a lesson' and prevent the other villagers from sheltering resistance fighters in the future. If you refuse to obey his order, the colonel will almost certainly tell his soldiers to shoot you and all the hostages. Sometimes, however, soldiers are not prepared to follow such ruthless commands, especially if you had done what was ordered and killed the two guerrillas, so you might be able to call the colonel's bluff. Given all these uncertainties, what is the right thing for you to do?

Here is a range of the reasons you might give for making your decision. Firstly, you may reckon that your best hope of saving at least some lives is to kill the remaining two guerrillas, since that way only two more lives will be lost rather than more than 80 (*if* the colonel keeps his promise). On the other hand, you may believe that murder is absolutely wrong and refuse to bludgeon to death the two bound men in front of you. Or you may see it as your duty as mayor not to give in to the vicious actions of the occupying force, but to set an example by defying the order – and perhaps try to use the empty gun to strike down the colonel!

Now, imagine you are one of the colonel's soldiers with your machine gun trained on the villagers. Would you obey his order to shoot them? Examples of reasons given for obeying are: a soldier's duty is to obey orders without question; or, you need to avoid the dire consequences for yourself of mutiny. Examples of reasons given for disobeying are: you would refuse to obey an unjust or immoral order (if the colonel orders the mass shooting even when the mayor obeys); or you are simply incapable of shooting down defenceless civilians, orders or not.

Although this scenario has nothing explicitly to do with bioethics, it does serve to highlight the ways in which different moral theories might suggest methods for dealing with the dilemmas encountered in bioethics. So, in the following sections of this chapter, I shall look at five different types of theory, all of which can be related to the kinds of reasons for decisions provoked by the mayor's dilemma.

COUNTING THE CONSEQUENCES

Many people will think that the obvious answer to the mayor's dilemma is to kill the prisoners, since only two lives will be taken (and they were going to die anyway) whilst 80 people will (perhaps) be spared death. It is often thought this is the common-sense – some would say, rational – approach to moral choice. The moral theory behind it is called **consequentialism**, and it can be summed up as requiring us to make moral decisions by judging past actions by their consequences and predicting as best we can the most probable consequences of prospective actions, seeking to maximize the good consequences and minimize the bad ones. The best-known consequentialist theory is **utilitarianism**, formulated first by the eighteenth- and nineteenth-century English philosopher and social reformer Jeremy Bentham. He devised the Greatest Happiness Principle, which stated that actions are right according to whether they produce the greatest amount of happiness and the least amount of pain for the greatest number of people. So, according to this theory, it seems obvious that the mayor's correct moral choice is to obey the colonel's order.

Consequentialism in various forms has had a major influence in bioethics and is probably still the dominant theory in the subject. The theory can sometimes appear attractive to health professionals, since it seems to reflect how they make their everyday clinical decisions, seeking to maximize benefit for their patients and to avoid, or minimize, harms. A well-known exponent of the approach is the Australian philosopher and first president of the IAB, Peter Singer, who has written across a wide range of topics, including use of animals, euthanasia, treatment of severely handicapped infants and our obligations to the poor. In these situations, Singer argues, we need to make our choices by seeking to minimize pain and suffering (including the suffering of non-human animals), in some cases at a cost, if need be, of ending lives.

Yet consequentialism is not as straightforward as it at first appears. The first problem is the uncertainty of predicting consequences. As we have seen, the colonel may shoot the hostages anyway. The mayor cannot be sure that killing two people will save the lives of 80. The uncertainty of consequences is also a feature of nearly all medicine and health care. For example, it used to be thought that giving premature infants high doses of oxygen would help them to survive and develop, but then it was discovered that this could cause blindness. Medicine must proceed by trial and error, and sometimes the cure can be worse than the disease. Consequentialists answer this problem by distinguishing between acts and rules. Clearly it may be difficult for anyone to predict all the consequences of one specific act, but instead we can rely on rules for conduct, forged over many years of human experience and known to promote the best consequences usually, but not necessarily in every case. So we should follow these rules and adapt them as the consequences of following them become clearer. This, of course, is how modern medicine normally deals with uncertainty. It relies on clinical research to give guidelines based on the best **evidence-based medicine**.

Then what would be the rule for the mayor? It is hard to know, but it might be the moral maxim 'do not kill'. By following this, the mayor might know that in this case it could bring terrible consequences, but that respecting it and not giving in to barbarity would be better for society in the long run. On the other hand, he might decide that the rule had to be broken in this situation, since this was more likely to save the larger number of lives. Yet, we have to keep saying 'might' in this discussion! The reality is that even rules forged over years of human experience cannot guarantee that our actions will bring the best consequences, whether in the long term or the short term. The consequentialist confidence that we have a simple solution to moral uncertainty seems somewhat misplaced. How do we know when rules, based on predicted consequences, should be broken?

And now we come to a second problem with consequentialism. How do we *define* the good and bad outcomes or consequences? Jeremy Bentham thought this was quite easy. We need to develop a 'felicific calculus', by which he meant a scientific measuring system for human happiness, which would allow us to estimate the quantity, fruitfulness, intensity and duration of pain and pleasure of any given action, and so work out which actions or social policies scored the highest. Of course, as Bentham's disciple (and unwilling critic), John Stuart Mill, soon perceived when he tried to defend the theory, trying to measure pain and pleasure fails to capture what constitutes human happiness or fulfilment. (It would be possible to make everyone happy, in a sense, by universally and surreptitiously administering a mood-changing drug – an idea explored in Aldous Huxley's *Brave New World*). Mill distinguished between 'higher' and 'lower' pleasures; and he recognized that there were certain human 'goods' that could not be reduced to a calculation of amounts of pleasure, but had value as ends in themselves. The chief example of such a human 'good' is liberty, but others include the search for knowledge and the appreciation of beauty.

So, we might ask concerning the mayor's dilemma, was not life under a brutal tyranny in fact worse than dying opposing it? The tragedy for the mayor was that he had to answer this impossible question not just for himself, but for all those whose lives he might perhaps save, only for them to suffer possibly years of vicious and sadistic imprisonment.

When we relate this second problem (defining good and bad outcomes) to bioethics, we find that it is a really tough one to solve. Of course, sometimes the beneficial outcomes of medicine and health care are obvious and easy to measure. In cases of serious and curable disease or recovery from accident, there is little doubt about what will be the best outcome. But, as the WHO has pointed out, health is often not simply 'the absence of disease or disability' (World Health Organization, 1948). A person may be dying or be seriously disabled, but live a life of greater fulfilment than those who live physically healthy, yet emotionally and spiritually discontented, lives. And often in medicine a choice has to be made between quantity and quality of life. Mere survival, but with unremitting pain, fear or indignity, may not be the outcome people would choose for themselves. Thus, such value questions, beyond the simple calculation of pleasure and pain, make it very hard to know for sure how consequences are to be used to help us make the right decisions.

There is also a third problem with consequentialism, which we can identify as the problem of justice. We can describe justice in terms of fairness to all, treating all persons with equal respect and without discrimination. Clearly, the scenario on the occupied island is one of gross injustice. No doubt in a time of war the guerrillas, as combatants, might be seen as justifiably executed, but the same cannot be said for the hostages. Since they were chosen at random from among the villagers, they cannot be rightly seen as co-conspirators with the resistance against the enemy forces. Obviously the colonel is using them as an example to scare off any future attempts at resistance. It does not matter to him if they all die, so long as he gets the result he wants; and the same will be true if he persuades the mayor, a representative public figure, to side with him in the execution of the prisoners. He is trying to force the mayor to collude with the injustice of threatening the innocent by accepting his terms for sparing the hostages. However, for consequentialism (except in a very sophisticated form which we shall discuss below) none of this matters, so long as more lives are saved than are lost. It may be important for people to be treated justly *usually*, since this will make for a happier society, but if the situation demands it, justice must be sacrificed.

We can relate this to bioethics by thinking of the origins of research ethics, described in the last chapter, in the Code which emerged from the Nuremberg trials. Suppose the horrific experimentation on concentration camp inmates had resulted in some major advances in therapeutic medicine (in fact they did not produce any outcomes of this kind, apart from some findings about hypothermia coming from freezing people to death). Would these agonizing deaths of a few people be justified by the saving of thousands of lives in the future? If the majority benefit can be enhanced in this way, what is there in the consequentialist account that marks it out as wrong? A rule-consequentialist might respond in terms of the undermining of a sense of security in society. If such acts were permitted, the argument goes, then people would never know when they might become the next victim for the common good. Thus the general happiness would not be served by permitting the abuse of a few for majority benefit.

But let us imagine a scenario where such majority-benefiting injustices are unlikely to be discovered. An example given by Griffin (1997) imagines surgeons operating on a man who lives a solitary life and has become cut off from all family and friends. They realize that he has a set of healthy organs which could save the lives of several needy patients, so, rather than making sure that he survives, they 'accidentally' allow him to die on the operating table, and then salvage his organs. Since no one will be made to feel insecure, provided the actions go undetected, and since several lives are saved, what are the consequentialist grounds for describing this action as morally wrong? A similar argument might be made for justifying capital punishment on consequentialist grounds, since executed criminals could provide a steady supply of organs for transplantation and most members of society would not expect to be in the same situation, and might see them to be worthy of death. Indeed, the security of society might be enhanced by the knowledge that dangerous criminals would not be free to threaten society again. Yet surely there is something unjust in relating the execution of convicted criminals to the supply of organs for transplantation. If demand for organs continued to increase, should we take steps to achieve an increase in executions?

So, perhaps we should conclude that consequentialism, despite its common-sense appearance, is not up to the task of helping to deal with the issues arising in bioethics. But this would be a rather hasty conclusion. The attempt to predict the likely outcomes of individual actions and policy decisions in bioethics must always be one feature of a carefully reasoned approach. If we don't try our best to establish all the relevant facts and to make well-informed predictions about consequences, then we could be at the mercy of what some writers have called the 'yuk factor' in ethics – a reaction of distaste or disapproval, based solely on emotion and unexamined prejudice. On the other hand, the simplistic notion that it is easy to put values on different consequences, even if we are able to be reasonably sure of them, also needs radical criticism. What is needed is a more nuanced account of social benefit and of human fulfilment. Only when we know more about the key human values to be defended and promoted are we likely to have an adequate way of assessing whether individual choices and social policies have genuine moral worth. This enrichment of consequentialist calculations is offered by some of the other approaches to ethics that I will now discuss, in preparation for a suggested way forward in using moral theory in bioethics.

DOING ONE'S DUTY

Let us return to the scene in the village square, but this time start with the soldiers, whose machine guns are trained on the hostages. In one possible outcome, the mayor does as he is told and kills the guerrillas, but then the colonel orders his men to shoot the 80 hostages anyway. How will the soldiers react? As soldiers, their first duty is to obey orders, but one or more of them may refuse to shoot. Why? One answer will be that they are not obliged to obey an immoral command. This is a dilemma that has been faced in real life in many war situations. A notorious example was the My Lai massacre on 16 March 1968 during the Vietnam War. Between 300 and 500 Vietnamese civilians, mostly women, children (including some babies) and elderly people were tortured, raped, murdered and mutilated by a US army platoon under the command of Second Lieutenant William Calley. Three US servicemen who tried to halt the massacre were denounced by a US senator, received hate mail, and were not honoured for their bravery until 30 years after the event. Calley served three-and-a-half years of what was originally a life sentence, merely under house arrest.

The soldiers' possible refusal to obey an immoral order opens up a very different kind of moral theory, one that sees an absolute requirement to do one's *moral duty*, whatever the consequences. This approach to moral decision making is known as **deontological theory** (from the Greek word *deon* − 'it is required'). Its most powerful exponent was the eighteenth-century German philosopher Immanuel Kant. Kant drew a distinction between what he called '**hypothetical imperatives**' and '**categorical imperatives**'. The first type of imperative lays down the requirements for achieving some desired end. An example would be: 'If you want to remain healthy, exercise regularly and eat a sensible diet'. Obviously, you need not obey this imperative if you don't see the end result, health, as one of your priorities. So, you may prefer a life of TV watching and eating fast food, realizing that your health may suffer, but thinking that you will at least die happy! In contrast with this conditional obedience of hypothetical imperatives, a **categorical imperative** requires unconditional obedience and overrides our preferences and desires. According to Kant, it does not depend on your having certain desires at all, but solely on knowing your duty and following it, whatever the consequences. In fact, Kant thought that the best sign that we were following our duty was when we did something we did *not* want to do. A soldier disobeying an order at the peril of his or her own life would be a good example of this.

How, then, do we know what our moral duty is? Kant offered several answers to this question. The first was based on the idea of universal law, which would apply to everyone in the same circumstances, without exception or partiality. So, when considering a particular action, we must ask ourselves, can I consistently will that this same action be done by others, when I am at the receiving end of the action? For example, if I think it would be all right for me to tell a lie when circumstances warrant it, can I also agree that it is all right that I will be lied to at times? (I shall return to this lying example later.) Kant thought that we would quickly see the illogicality of this idea, and recognize that the prohibition of lying must be absolute, otherwise we could never be sure of when people are being truthful. This test of moral consistency is probably familiar to most of us, in the form of what is called the Golden Rule: 'Do unto others as you would have done unto you'.

A second account of the categorical imperative offered by Kant can be summed up in the idea of the need to have a society in which there is collaboration and harmony among all moral agents. Kant called this being 'a member of a rational kingdom of ends'. We know we are doing our duty when following it enables and protects others also following their moral duty. Thus, together we ensure respect for the moral law throughout society. This prevents us from merely promoting our own personal ends and enables us to create a society in which all are equally respected and honoured. This formulation leads on to the third and best-known version of Kant's categorical imperative, which can be summed up in the phrase 'respect for persons'. Kant's wording is: 'So act as to treat humanity, whether in your own person or that of any other, in every case as an end, never a mere means.'

Now perhaps we can see the force of this theory in demanding a moral stand against evil and injustice and promoting a defence of human rights. In the village scenario the hostages are treated as 'mere means' to the ends of the occupying force. They have no value in themselves, no right to life or freedom from fear, no say in their own fate. For any soldier who disobeys the order to shoot, the consequences will be dire, so his or her only motive must be moral (rather than military) duty, a refusal to compromise with evil and condone injustice. A similar commitment to the moral imperative may lead the mayor to disobey the colonel, though his dilemma is more acute, since he may fear that refusing to kill will merely add to the death toll. But Kant would say that he must disobey the colonel, that the only certainty is the moral law. Counting possible consequences can never tell us our duty.

So how useful is this theory for the dilemmas of bioethics? Thinking back again to the notorious uses of humans as experimental guinea pigs, it is clear that the Kantian injunction never to treat people as mere means prohibits such actions absolutely. When the US government gave immunity from war crimes prosecution to the Japanese doctors doing research into biological weapons so that it could get the data (ostensibly for defence purposes) (Harris, 1994), it treated the Chinese prisoners who suffered agonizing deaths as no more than convenient sources for information that it believed to be essential for its own country's national security. Moreover, duty-based ethics has an effect much wider than the proscription of such obvious compromises with evil. The centrality of moral agency in the theory has led to a revolution in the way medical ethics has been understood. The idea of 'the patient as a person' has become normative in all aspects of the therapeutic relationship, resulting in a new emphasis on **autonomous** choice by patients, which affects key aspects of medical care, such as communication, confidentiality and treatment decisions. We shall return to these in detail in Chapter 4, but at this stage we can see that an approach to ethics that accords to every person an equal moral status is a powerful weapon against arrogance, paternalism and the abuse of professional power.

Yet, despite these advantages, this theory does leave us with some puzzles and problems. The first of these is that it seems to promise too much by way of moral certainty. Is our duty always as clear as is suggested by the theory, and is it really the case that all moral rules are absolute, allowing for no exceptions? For example, Kant believed that it was always our duty to tell the truth, whatever the consequences, and that allowing exceptions would invalidate the nature of truth itself. In his own writing, he imagines a scene in which a murderer is pursuing his victim and this person has taken refuge in our house. Must we tell the murderer the truth when he comes knocking at our door? Yes, says Kant, for we cannot be sure that lying will bring good consequences – it could in fact bring bad ones, since the person may have already escaped from a window and our lie would send the assassin in his direction! Our duty is to be truthful and to face the consequences, including defending the victim from the killer if need be.

Yet, is this somewhat extreme conclusion really necessary? Kant's idea that any lie will undercut the veracity of all communication seems to ignore the sophistication of human interactions. We can quite often distinguish between a habitually deceitful person, whose word we would never trust, and a trustworthy person, who may sometimes have to conceal the truth for the sake of more important moral ends (Bok, 1978). Numerous examples can be used to illustrate this, from relatively trivial ones (the 'white lie' to avoid hurting a friend's feelings) to very serious ones (captured soldiers who lie under interrogation to save the lives of others).

This leads us to an unresolved problem in Kant's absolutist approach. Duties conflict at times, and not all of them can be met in some situations. In the above example, the duty to protect life conflicts with the duty to tell the truth. So it seems better to talk about *prima facie* ('on the face of it') duties, realizing that there is more work to do in order to decide what any particular situation requires of us. Let us take some medical examples to illustrate this. In one case, a young person needs a kidney transplant and the best result would come from a living related donor, whose blood type is compatible, so there will be less risk of rejection. The brother of the patient is tested and is a match for the recipient, but he tells the doctor in confidence that (although he is ashamed of this) he is really too frightened to go through with the operation. He does not want his family to know this. The doctor tells the family that the potential donor is 'not compatible'. Is this lie morally justified? Is it really a lie, or just 'economy with the truth', since the doctor has not said *why* the donor is incompatible? In a second case, the tests done to establish compatibility reveal that the donor is not in fact the child of both parents. Does the doctor have a duty to reveal this information to the parents, to him, to all three, or to none of them? The Kantian answer seems unambiguous – the truth must be told to all parties. But is this really the doctor's duty? And is deciding not to reveal some information exactly the same as a direct lie or deception?

These dilemmas reveal that Kant's idea that we always have a clear test of whether an imperative is categorical does not really work in practice. It is obviously important to see the force of moral rules. They are not just matters of convention or convenience, not just to be followed when we feel like it and ignored when they frustrate our desires. But they do not come in the simple, unconditional form suggested by Kant: Do not kill; do not lie; always keep promises; and so on. In these formulations they cannot be made into universal moral laws, as Kant believed. The Golden Rule, that we should do unto others as we would have done unto ourselves, may be a good test of the impartiality of our decisions, but it does not tell us enough about what is morally required. For example, I might prefer that people lie to me about whether I have terminal cancer, but that does not mean that I can make it into a universal rule for everyone in my situation. Agreeing to do this as a moral requirement may depend on the circumstances of each case. Similarly, we can agree that killing is wrong in most circumstances, but still, without obvious contradiction, recognize that it could be our duty to kill (for example, to prevent a mass murderer continuing to fire on innocent bystanders). Our moral absolutes need to be more carefully formulated.

We can perhaps make more progress by using Kant's alternative formulation of the basic moral law: always treat people (including ourselves) as ends in themselves, never as mere means to an end. Here we need to note that the prohibition is on treating people as *mere* means. We treat people as means to our ends all the time: the bus driver is the means of our reaching a lecture hall in time; the lecturer is a means of our learning more about an interesting or useful subject; if we get sick, the doctors and other health professionals are a means to our recovery; our sexual partners can be a means for us to have children of our own. However, if these are morally acceptable relationships, all these people have chosen to help us to achieve our ends. The bus driver, lecturer and health professionals have chosen to provide the services we receive and are remunerated for it; and, if our sexual partner has not consented to having a child by us, but is the victim of non-consensual sex or has been deceived by us (say, about contraception), then we have treated him or her as mere means to get a child. Thus, at the core of this basic moral principle, is the requirement to respect the **autonomy** of others. Later I shall discuss this concept in more detail, but for the present we can see it as allowing people to make their own moral choices, to direct their own lives in ways that they believe to be right, to be – in a phrase – free moral agents.

We can now see, using this Kantian formula, that there are some moral absolutes. Slavery in all its forms, rape and other unprovoked physical assaults, murder, exploitation, deception for personal gain and the betrayal of trust, especially the trust of the vulnerable, are unconditionally wrong. In all these cases, people are used as mere objects to serve the purposes of others. They have been deprived of some or all of the most basic of all human attributes, the capacity to make their own choices about those things which matter to them in life, planning their own futures and living with the consequences of those choices. At this most basic level of moral reasoning, Kant seems to be absolutely right. But the devil is in the detail, as we shall see later on. Knowing about these moral absolutes does not automatically enable us to get the day-to-day moral rules neatly wrapped up in the orderly way Kant hoped to achieve.

There is one other problem with Kant's approach: his rationalistic account of moral agency. We have seen already that he puts rationality at the centre of morality. His concept of a moral law was one which could be accepted as universal by all *rational beings*; and in another formulation, as we saw above, he spoke of a *rational* kingdom of ends. In the same way, his distinction between hypothetical and categorical imperatives depends on a radical separation of feelings or desires, on the one side, and reason, on the other. For Kant, feelings will lead us astray; only the strict exercise of reason will enable us to both know and obey the moral law. (His only concession to emotion was to say that we would be helped to act morally by feeling 'respect' for the moral law, which he described as a kind of awe similar to the feelings generated by the 'starry heavens above'.)

However, this creates two difficulties for an adequate account of what is entailed in moral choices. Requiring logical reasoning (which is what Kant seems to mean by rationality) seems to be asking both too much of us and too little. It is asking too much because it would suggest that only those humans who possess such analytical powers can be seen as part of his community of moral agents, and this would surely exclude all children and those humans who do not possess the level of intelligence that he seems to demand. Does this mean that such people do not merit the respect accorded to moral agents? If so, then it would seem to be morally acceptable to treat them as mere means, even perhaps enslaving them if this served the ends of the members of the rational elite. (Children might be exempted, since they may eventually attain the rationality required.) Of course, Kant probably did not intend such a conclusion (so far as we know), but the logic of his position seems to be that the boundaries of the human family extend only so far as rationality of the quality that he requires can be demonstrated. This would have serious repercussions for bioethics, implying, for example, that we do not have to have the same standards of treatment for those with **cognitive impairments** as we would require for those of 'normal' intelligence.

A second difficulty with the concentration on rationality is that it seems to miss some essential features of the moral life. It is asking too little of us. We know from experience that highly intelligent people are *not* always the most admirable morally! They can use their reason in a cold and calculating way, perhaps to further their own advantage, or, when they do consider others, being helpful out of an impersonal sense of duty, obeying the letter but not the spirit of the law. Such duty-driven individuals can be hard to bear.

Thus Kant, with his stress on an iron-clad rational duty, seems to ask too little by suggesting that the ability to see logical contradictions or inconsistencies in our actions is enough to ensure that we act morally. But we look for far more than this in moral agents, and this 'more' is in the realm of emotion, not reason. We look for empathy, compassion and a certain humility that sees the limits of our wisdom and the fallibility of our decision making. To put it simply: we sense that in order to get right actions, we need good people. So it is to this idea – that morality is what good people do – that I now turn.

BEING A GOOD PERSON – VIRTUE ETHICS

My discussion of the limitations of Kant's emphasis on duty, based in rationality, takes us to another major tradition in ethical theory, **virtue ethics** (VE). This approach can be traced back to the ancient Greeks, with a major exponent being the philosopher and natural scientist Aristotle, but it also found its way into the Christian tradition when mediaeval theologians began to make lists of virtues and vices. It has seen a revival recently, reflecting a dissatisfaction with the way both consequentialist and deontological approaches deal with the moral life. The VE approach can be summed up by a comparison with these theories, which seek answers to the question, 'What should I *do*?' In contrast with this stress on difficult choices, VE asks a different question, 'How shall I *be*?' or, 'What sort of life should I lead?' Thus the focus is shifted from the individual choices or decisions made by people in challenging situations to the enduring character of moral agents.

Returning to the horrifying scene in the village square, we can sense the fear and nausea anyone must feel as he or she sees the mutilated corpses of those already executed. This is where the so called 'yuk factor' is important in morality, since it makes us recoil from the sheer inhumanity with which some people treat others. Yet just reacting emotionally to such scenes will never be enough in guiding us to the right moral decision. If you are a health professional, you will no doubt remember times when you had to find strength in the face of horrific scenes of suffering and death, scenes which required you to develop a professional attitude, yet retain your natural horror at the sight before you. Too much emotional involvement means that you cannot act effectively: but too little, and you become detached and uncaring.

This was the emotional turmoil confronting the mayor as he was ordered to join in the callous brutality before his eyes by clubbing the other two prisoners to death. You may have felt when you considered your choice that you could never do what the colonel was trying to make you do. You simply could not obey the order. This is not just that you may believe that all killing is wrong, but that, whatever the stakes, you could never do such a thing, could not live with the memory of having done it. (Others, of course, will say the opposite, that they could not live with the guilt of having caused the death of so many hostages.) This powerful sense that one cannot collude with inhumanity and injustice might also be felt by the soldiers, especially if they are told to shoot after the mayor has obeyed the colonel's order. Again, this is not just that the act is breaking some moral rule – it is simply not the kind of thing that that person could ever do. They cannot live such a life and be true to themselves.

It is this blend of reason and emotion, acting as a guide to our actions throughout our lives, that VE is seeking to capture. There is, however, no single theory of VE but, rather, a cluster of theories, which have both similarities and differences. One thing they have in common is the attempt to base ethics on the essential elements of human nature – to see ethics as an expression of our true humanity. It is here that the central notion of 'virtue' comes in. To modern ears, the word sounds like a description of special people, of heroes or saints (Nelson Mandela or Mother Teresa), well above the level of common humanity. But this is not what the Greek word for virtue (*arete*) means. It expresses simply the essential function of anything. So, the virtue of a knife (a 'good' knife) is that it cuts well. (In the hands of a surgeon it can cure, and in the hands of a murderer it can kill, but in either case it retains its virtue, if it cuts well.) So, virtuous human beings are not exceptional people, but simply ordinary people who are true to their own nature, who act in a humane way.

What, then, is our true nature? It is here that the various theories diverge. The classical theory, going back to Aristotle, sees two forms of virtue, intellectual and moral. The intellectual virtues reflect our nature as rational animals, but consist of more than simply skill in logical reasoning. In addition to the type of reasoning that helps us make scientific discoveries and technical innovations, we are endowed with a kind of practical wisdom (*sophrosune* in Greek) which grows with experience and enables us to make considered moral choices. The moral virtues supplement this intellectual ability. They are a blend of reason and emotion, habitual ways of acting, developed by experience and training from childhood, which give balance and harmony to our lives and to our relationships with others. These moral virtues are characterized by the 'golden mean', a proper balance between deficiency and excess. Thus, as an example, courage is a moral virtue, and its corresponding vices are cowardice (deficiency) and rashness (excess). Courage maintains a balance between these extremes. In a similar way, temperance is the golden mean between gluttony and asceticism. In addition to courage and temperance, other 'cardinal' virtues are prudence and justice. To these four virtues Christian tradition added three 'theological' virtues: faith, hope and love – and then added seven corresponding vices (or 'deadly sins') for good measure!

So the traditional answer to the question – 'How shall I live?' – is that we must nourish these virtues and avoid the corresponding vices. However, such list making can seem somewhat arbitrary and unhelpful. Is there some kind of unifying theme running through these descriptions that enables us to say of a person that they are a good person, someone we can trust to make good decisions and live in helpful relationships with others? Modern VE theorists have tried to describe such a unified theme in human virtue in terms of realistically facing up to the challenges of being human. This will mean accepting our vulnerability as living creatures and our inevitable dependency on others at different phases of our lives; it will acknowledge our need to find some sense of meaning and purpose in our lives; and, finally, it will enable us to confront our mortality, coming to terms with the knowledge that we, and those we love, must all, some day, die. Pulling this all together is a sense of self-fulfilment (called by the Greeks *eudaimonia*, literally 'having a good spirit'); this comes from the knowledge that our lives have been worthwhile and, despite some failures, have brought some goodness into the lives of others. Another term to sum up this idea of the fulfilment of our capacities as humans is 'human flourishing', and this can be contrasted with the denial of the human potential for goodness in acts of selfishness, violence and despair.

There are several ways in which VE can be related to bioethics. The most frequent way has been to try to describe the 'virtuous practitioner', a health professional whom patients can trust and who provides a good role model for students and trainees. This can be helpful in practice and is clearly relevant to professional education, in which the 'hidden curriculum' of peer pressure and models of practice by senior practitioners are well known to have a greater effect than the ideals of professionalism promulgated in lectures. But the danger here is a kind of glorification of the professions, putting them on a pedestal above the lay public, as though they hold a monopoly on ethical ideals. (This is the danger of elitism in VE, to which I return below.)

By way of counterbalance, we need to think more carefully about what might be meant by 'virtuous patients'. From the professional perspective, this term has often been used to describe patients who are compliant, uncomplaining and cheerful in adversity, and who never question medical judgement – in other words, the easy patient! However, the more modern account of VE, described above, offers a quite different perspective. It suggests patients as moral teachers of those caring for them, as they show us how to cope with human frailty and with the challenges of illness, disability and the fear of imminent death. The courage, perseverance and kindness of patients can often present a richer account of what it means to be human than can any medical heroics by health professionals.

VE is also relevant to bioethics because of its emphasis on the whole moral life rather than on incidents of moral choice and dilemma. In Chapter 1 we saw how, under the influence of the WHO, the social, political and environmental correlates of health have come increasingly into focus. Instead of being caught in the disease model of health, in which the dramas of acute medicine function prominently, bioethics has begun tackling issues of health care delivery, environmental causes of ill-health and those aspects of social life which foster or destroy healthy human development from birth to death. The weakness of the consequentialist and deontological approaches to ethics has been their portrayal of morality as a series of isolated moral choices – the 'what should I do?' question. VE opens up our horizons, helping us to consider the quality of our lives as a whole, both individually and socially.

It suggests that, unless we are willing to tackle the difficult questions about the purpose and value of human life, we are unlikely to know what the right decisions are. Thus we seem to have a richer theory for dealing with the complexities of the issues raised in contemporary bioethics.

However, like the other two theories, VE is not without its problems. The first, already referred to above, is that, despite its claims to be describing the ordinary capacities of all humans, it may be in fact both elitist and utopian. Is it reasonable to expect everyone to find self-fulfilment, to believe that they have had a meaningful life, to find ways of helping others and to face death with equanimity? Much of this may be to do with what has been called 'moral luck' (Nagel, 1979). We noted that the development of moral character is a matter of training and habituation from early years, but, then, what of those whose childhood has been one of deprivation, parental neglect and an environment of crime and violence? It is obvious that people vary greatly in their upbringing, in their life experiences and possibly also in inherited traits of character. So why should we expect that the norm for everyone is to live a life of harmony with others, to find fulfilment in what they do and to die a 'good death'? Is it not enough that we avoid causing serious harm to others, or, if we do, that we can make amends for it? And there is a further risk in such idealism. Notions of the 'good life' can be very class related and influenced by those in power. Is the good life manifested by an Oxford don or a Nottingham coal miner? Is it, in the manner of Lord Reith (the first Director General of the BBC), to be graced by the best in classical music and in political analysis, or can a good night in the pub suffice? How are we to distinguish matters of taste from those attributes which describe fundamental human goodness?

These are serious questions, especially if those in power take it upon themselves to impose their values on the society and give no scope for a range of conceptions of the good. History is full of examples of such an imposition of value, from Plato's plan in *The Republic* to expel poets from his ideal society, to the Communist and other ideologically based states of our era. This is a problem to which I will return in the next section, when describing **communitarian** ethics, but for the moment we can note that, while VE's stress on the goodness of people, which underpins the rightness of actions, is welcomed, we need to be cautious! It is one thing to try to have a vision of the good human life: it is quite another to impose it on others.

This leads us to the second problem with VE, already implied above: its account of 'virtues' and 'vices' can seem very culturally relative. Aristotle's model for the virtuous person was clearly a free Athenian man. Women, slaves and foreigners were not in the frame! Subsequently VE has fallen under powerful cultural influences, most notably Christianity with the adaptations of Aristotle's account by the mediaeval theologian Thomas Aquinas. In our own day many of the philosophers involved in the revival of VE have come from a Catholic Christian background. This is not in itself a problem, provided the arguments in favour of the theory do not involve a buy-in to the particular cultural or faith assumptions. Thus we could see force in Aristotle's account of the Golden Mean, without accepting his sexist and racist prejudices. Similarly, it is obvious that the Christian concept of other-regarding love (*agape*) is one of the influences on the more modern accounts of virtues such as justice and compassion, but this is not a difficulty if such a virtue is attainable without the need for divine intervention or religious faith.

We need to stress that cultural influence is not the same as cultural imperialism. Whatever the source of the ideas, the key question is whether they can be generalized to apply to humans in all cultures. In our era this question of generalizability has become even more pressing because of mass communications and the globalization of so many enterprises. It is no longer possible to keep ethical issues in some kind of cultural cocoon when the entire world can perceive, and be affected by, the events in our own society. The most obvious signs of this quest for some kind of broad account of basic human values are the UN Declaration of Human Rights, drawn up after the Second World War and the increasing activities of war crime tribunals, which have to appeal to fundamental humanitarian standards. We cannot escape entirely our own culture any more than we can jump out of our own skins, but we can try to find ways of transcending it. Maybe a genuinely universal VE can help us to do this.

A third criticism of VE is that it is too vague to give clear answers to the ethical dilemmas that we will encounter in bioethics and, more generally, in ethics. All that the theory tells us is that we must act as a virtuous person would act in the situation – but that hardly seems to be an answer at all! In the case of the mayor, we would surely count him virtuous whichever way he decided. He was clearly a well-intentioned, caring man, who wanted to do the best he could in an impossible situation. Some might admire him more for trying to save the hostages, others for refusing to compromise with evil, but surely no one would call him vicious. This criticism of VE does seem to hit its target. In fact, the theory does not claim to tell us what to do in specific situations. Its aim is to set the right context for such decision making, to help develop the sort of people who can be relied on to make the right decisions most of the time, and to foster a society in such a humanitarian attitude is common. That is why many writers have suggested that we need both VE and one of the decision-based theories to give us a complete picture of how to assess and guide moral actions. The question then comes down to which of the theories – consequentialist or deontological – will prove the best ally of VE. I shall be returning to this question later, but first we need to consider two other contenders for the position of the best normative theory: communitarian ethics and libertarian ethics. Assessing their adequacy will occupy me for the next two sections of this chapter, before I try to draw some tentative conclusions.

BROTHERHOOD AND SISTERHOOD – COMMUNITARIANISM

The rallying cry of the French Revolution was *Liberté, Egalité, Fraternité* (Liberty, Equality, Fraternity). It is the third of these, 'brotherhood', that communitarian ethics hopes to achieve (but I have sought sexual equality in my section heading!). Another, non-gender-specific, term is solidarity or social solidarity. In this approach the main criterion is whether the actions and decisions of individuals ensure the good of society. The individual will must be subservient to the general will and, indeed, a person's own good can be served only when the good of society is also served. This idea goes back to Aristotle, who famously described man as a 'political animal', whose nature it was to live in society. He went on: 'he who is unable to live in society or has no need because he is sufficient for himself must be either a beast or a god' (*Nichomachean Ethics*, Book 1, chapter 2). The eighteenth-century French philosopher Jean-Jacques Rousseau developed this idea further in his book, *The Social Contract*. A true democracy, Rousseau believed, would be a one-party state, since political parties merely result in compromises between rival interest groups. Instead of such factional politics, the 'general will' should be established in a general assembly of all the people, each voting according to his own beliefs and not according to any party line. Once this will is established it must be followed by all, since this is the Will of the People.

As we look back at such an idea after two centuries in which totalitarian states have made their citizens bend to the 'will of the people' by force and by subterfuge, it must seem dangerously idealistic and, indeed, a charter for tyranny. Yet there are aspects of the philosophy that deserve closer inspection. Firstly, we need to think carefully about what we mean by the 'self'. It is clear that we are not isolated individuals, each living in a world of our own, within which we have complete control of our lives. On the contrary, our freedom to choose and to act is both constrained and enabled by the society in which we live. As the English political philosopher Thomas Hobbes put it, without society our lives would be 'solitary, poor, nasty, brutish, and short'. Without an ordered society we could not be the makers of our own destiny that we imagine ourselves to be. All our energies would be taken up simply by the struggle to survive in a hostile environment. But in addition what we see as our individuality, our personal identity is very largely the creation of all those social factors – family, neighbourhood, school, nation, historical epoch – that have filled our memories, formed our attitudes and offered us goals to strive for. This does not mean that we have no freedom of choice, that all our decisions and actions are wholly predetermined, but we have not chosen the scope of choices open to us, nor have we created the influences that will structure and influence our choices. For all these reasons, the character of the communities in which we live is a crucial factor in our moral agency. We have much less scope for choice than we imagine!

Arising from this fundamental feature of our lives, we can see the importance of the communitarian stress on social solidarity. The quality of our personal and private lives is intimately related to the nature of the society in which we live, and it is in our interests to make that community work for the benefit of all. But where some communitarian approaches get it wrong is in their monolithic approach to the common good, seeing this as promoted only by a single way of ordering society. Down that path lies totalitarianism and tyranny. Instead, we need to look for a diversity of communities serving different ends. Some may be related to neighbourhood concerns, others to the protection of vulnerable groups, others again to the promotion of justice on a national or international scale. The philosopher Karl Popper called this approach 'piecemeal engineering', and he saw it as a bulwark against 'the greatest and most urgent evils of society' (Popper, 1974).

When viewed in this light, communitarian ethics can enhance our approach to bioethical issues by stressing the social dimension of our potential solutions, and, as we shall see in a later chapter, it has particular force when we are considering justice in health care provision. It does not, however, provide the kind of comprehensive moral theory offered by the others we have already discussed. Nevertheless, we can also see its power in the village scenario. Part of the mayor's agony was his sense of responsibility as the leader of a community. He could not make the choice based merely on the value of his own life, or even on a calculation of the number of lives which he might save. Beyond these calculations lay the symbolic significance of the colonel's choice of him as the executioner of the guerrillas. He was being asked to be the representative of the whole village's rejection of the resistance movement and its total subservience to his will. We could not imagine a more graphic illustration of how our lives are tied up with the lives of others, how so few of our choices relate solely to our personal future, especially if we have positions of social responsibility. In the words of John Donne (originally written in 1642):

> No man is an *island*, entire of itself; every man is a piece of the *continent*, a part of the *main*.
>
> (Donne, 2002)

Yet, the threat to individuality in communitarian approaches remains strong. In the next chapter I shall be discussing a range of approaches to bioethics that depend on the cultural setting, social situation or religious beliefs of the individual to define the rightness of moral choices in bioethics. We shall have a chance then to think more fully about how we can achieve a balance between personal freedom and the demands of society. But, for now, let us look at an account which is in total opposition to any account of morality that undercuts personal freedom.

LIVE FREE OR DIE – LIBERTARIANISM

The heading for this section is the motto of the state of New Hampshire in New England, and it captures well the revolutionary origins of the USA. The 1776 Declaration of Independence stated:

> We hold these truths to be self-evident, that all men are created equal, that they are endowed by their Creator with certain inalienable rights, that among these are Life, Liberty and the Pursuit of Happiness.

This stress on rights, and particularly on liberty as an inalienable right, forms the foundation of an approach to ethics which can be called **libertarianism** or liberal individualism. The theory can be seen as the polar opposite of the one we have just summarized. It stresses the freedom of the individual from social control, putting strict limits on the extent to which the state or society can encroach upon the choices and decisions of the individual. As we saw earlier, one powerful advocate of this stress on the non-interference in individual lives was John Stuart Mill. Here is how he put it in his famous essay, *On Liberty*:

> the only purpose for which power can be rightfully exercised over any member of a civilized community, against his will, is to prevent harm to others. His own good, either physical or moral, is not a sufficient warrant ... Over himself, over his own body and mind, the individual is sovereign.
>
> (Mill, 2004, pp. 33–34)

This statement is often referred to as Mill's Harm Principle, and it is used as the basis for numerous practical conclusions in bioethics, for example, in relation to suicide, voluntary euthanasia, sexual preference (when minors are not involved) and reproductive decisions. It can also influence wider policy decisions, for example, in relation to scientific and technical innovations, where (it is alleged) no harm can be conclusively predicted. Examples would be reproductive **cloning, germline modification**, and techniques for **human enhancement**, including prolonging the human life span (see Chapters 4 and 5 for a discussion of these issues). A frequent target of this approach is what has been called the Precautionary Principle, which seeks to control individual choices and new social policies, for fear of possible, but uncertain, negative consequences. The libertarian has no time for such constraint!

In its more extreme forms, libertarianism severely limits the power of the state and sees no ethical obligations on us, apart from the defence of our individual rights. Thus taxation can be seen as a form of legalized robbery, and our moral responsibility does not extend to ensuring the welfare of others, since it is up to them to see to this for themselves. It would be hard to see how such a theory would help the mayor in his dilemma, apart from seeking the solution that would be least likely to curtail his own liberty. He no longer has any ethical obligations to the hostages or to the village as a whole, only to his own survival.

However, in its less extreme forms, this approach clearly has echoes of the Kantian stress on respect for autonomy. We can also – following the terminology of a more recent philosopher, Isaiah Berlin – distinguish two types of freedom, negative and positive. Mill's Harm Principle stresses *non-interference*. We are to be left to make our own choices, without any controls upon this, apart from not causing harm to others. This can be called 'negative freedom'. But what of conditions that will enrich people's powers of choice? This would not entail imposing a way of life on people (as communitarianism may be in danger of doing), but giving them a wider range of possibilities from which to choose. This we may call 'positive freedom'. If we grant the importance of this aspect of freedom, then in the name of greater freedom for individuals we can embark on projects designed to improve the quality of people's lives, without jeopardizing the fundamental value of individual choice (Berlin, 1958).

In this revised version of liberal theory, there is room for a richer account of moral agency than the highly individualistic version allows. If we see autonomy not as mere randomness of choice ('doing what I feel like'), but, rather, as commitment to a set of self-chosen, not externally imposed, values, then improving human health and well-being becomes a project to enhance autonomy. There is both an individual and a social obligation to achieve this both for ourselves and for others. The pursuit of liberty for all equally, in the spirit of the US Declaration of Independence, need not entail discarding the fundamental importance of achieving a society in which freedom flourishes. When this is related to bioethics, we can see that the challenge of libertarianism is that it forces us to think more deeply about the meaning of both autonomy and justice. For example, the notion of health as a fundamental human right can be related to the critical relationship between human freedom and health. If we do not take steps to remove the barriers to individual capabilities that are so evident in societies without universal provision of health and welfare services, then the claim to be defending human freedom is truly empty rhetoric. (In Chapter 6 I return to this issue in greater depth.)

A BALANCING ACT – THE FOUR PRINCIPLES

What, then, are we to make of the range of theory described in this chapter? How are we to make sense of it in a way that will really help us with the problems discussed in bioethics? The answer could lie in seeking some kind of balance between the different emphases they represent, recognizing that each has both strengths and weaknesses. This is the approach taken in *Principles of Biomedical Ethics* by Tom Beauchamp and James Childress (2012). They believe that we can identify a common morality across human cultures to which all humans can subscribe, and that in this common morality we can identify four broad principles which serve as a suitable starting point for biomedical ethics. The principles are: respect for autonomy; non-maleficence; beneficence; and justice.

We shall see in more detail what Beauchamp and Childress mean by these terms, but first we need to note a common mis-understanding and misuse of these principles. The authors make it clear that they do *not* provide some kind *formula* for solving moral problems. They simply offer a way of structuring the kinds of questions that must be confronted when facing moral problems in bioethics. Much more work is needed to see how they each can help in specific situations. However, health professionals are used to handy formulas and guidelines for dealing with clinical situations, for example, the mnemonic ABCDE, standing for 'airway, breathing, circulation, drugs, environment', is used as check-list in emergency life support. The four principles are often cited in clinical ethics discussions, as though they somehow give this kind of guidance. For this reason they have been nick-named the 'Georgetown Mantra', after Georgetown University, where Beauchamp works. But this is not at all how the authors intend them to function. Instead, they see the need for some kind of balance or 'reflective equilibrium' (a phrase borrowed from the legal philosopher John Rawls) between the principles, with much more specification needed to make them useful in the wide range of situations encountered in bioethics. In addition, they do not claim that there is any significance in the order of the principles, and this is especially important, since they have been accused of giving priority to respect for autonomy over the other three. Let us, then, see how each of the principles might help in the attempt to apply theory to practice in bioethics.

AUTONOMY

We are already familiar with this concept from the brief account of Kant's theory earlier and also from Mill's stress on personal liberty. Beauchamp and Childress stress that respect for autonomy entails more than simply an attitude of toleration of others' choices: it must also entail action to ensure that the capacity of others to make choices is both defended and enhanced. However, they differ from Kant in his belief in a universal moral law to which all rational beings will subscribe. Instead they are closer to Mill's idea of ensuring that people are free to act according to their personal values and beliefs, provided this does not cause harm to others. Later, we shall see how this needs to be spelled out in detail when medical decisions are made about treatment or non-treatment, confidentiality and public health policies.

NON-MALEFICENCE AND BENEFICENCE

The second principle goes back to an ancient medical maxim, *Primum non nocere* ('first of all, do no harm'). Its connection to the requirements of research ethics is obvious, but it also applies more widely to medical practice (the participation of doctors in torture, for example) and, more widely still, to policies which hazard human health (industrial pollution, destruction of the environment and global warming). Beauchamp and Childress restrict the scope of their discussion to medical practice, but, as we are looking at bioethics as a whole, we shall need to include these wider socio-political questions.

Clearly, the principle of beneficence is closely related to non-maleficence, the prohibition of harm, but this principle stresses a positive requirement to do good to others (not to be confused with 'benevolence', which is merely a willingness to do good, or an attitude of goodwill towards others). In practicing beneficence we do not merely refrain from harming others, we try to prevent harm to them, to remove that which is harmful, to counterbalance any harm with benefit, and actively to promote their well-being. This can be seen as the principal aim of medicine and health care, and the failure to act beneficently as a betrayal of the trust which patients place in the good intentions of health professionals. Obviously, the practice of medicine can often entail harm, for example, the use of powerful drugs for treating cancer, which can have toxic side-effects, and, for this reason, the ratio of benefit to harm becomes crucial.

A hazard in the principle of beneficence is what has been labelled as 'paternalism' in health care. A strong form of paternalism entails imposing treatment on people 'for their own good', even when they do not wish to receive it. In exploring this hazard we will see that there is clearly no simple formula, since acting in this way, while perhaps satisfying the beneficence principle, breaches respect for autonomy. Both cannot be satisfied, so a choice between them must be made.

JUSTICE

The fourth principle, justice, creates more potential for conflict. We already saw how consequentialist calculations (which clearly underlie the non-maleficence and beneficence principles) provoke major problems of justice or fairness. If all persons are to be treated with equal respect and consideration according to their needs, then it will not be morally acceptable to maximize the benefit of any one individual, or even of the majority in the society, if doing so will result in the unfair treatment of others. For example, a very expensive treatment might be available which could save the lives of some patients, but, since resources for health care will always be limited, providing it to some could jeopardize the treatment and even the survival of others with different needs for heath care. Distributing benefits and costs fairly, which is one of the basic features of justice, demands a different and more demanding form of moral reasoning than simply working out potential benefits and harms to individuals.

KEEPING OUR BALANCE

So can the Four Principles approach of Beauchamp and Childress help us at all in our need to find a way through the dilemmas of bioethics? If properly understood, it probably can. We have already noticed that it is easily misunderstood and misused. The principles can help us to formulate the relevant questions (or most of them), but they do not provide the answers to specific dilemmas. To do this, we need to be aware of the moral issues at stake in each situation and then draw on the richness of the various moral theories available to us. We need to ask questions like, are we justified in overruling individual choice in these circumstances for the sake of a more just outcome? Which decision will create the best ratio of benefit to harm to those affected? What is our duty in this situation and how does it relate to the fundamental values of our society, such as respect for the rights of all persons?

If this seems a somewhat precarious way of doing ethics, one sadly lacking in the kind of quick and definite conclusions that would get us back down to solid ground, we at least have the consolation of knowing that others whom we respect and admire also struggle to get the balance right. The most dangerous practitioners, whether of medicine or of morality, are those who never know what it feels like to be uncertain. And this takes us back to VE – somewhere in that middle ground between deficiency and excess we will find the kind of practical wisdom that we need. In the chapters that follow, we will see how this spells out in detailed decision making across the range of issues in bioethics.

FURTHER READING

For more information about the philosophical theories covered in this chapter see Nigel Warburton's book in this series, *Philosophy: The Basics* (2012). For a discussion of Kant's ethics as it relates to bioethics you should turn to Onora O'Neill's excellent book, *Autonomy and Trust in Bioethics* (2002). There are essays on most of the other theories in Ashcroft, Dawson, Draper et al., *Principles of Health Care Ethics* (2007). For VE (and also care ethics, which is discussed in the next chapter) see my essay 'The "ethics of care" as virtue ethics', in Evans (1998, pp. 295–305). If you want to understand Principlism, rather than 'pop' versions of it, you should read Tom Beauchamp's essay in Ashcroft, Dawson, Draper et al., or else consult the latest edition of *Principles of Biomedical Ethics* (2012). For Internet searches on philosophical concepts and theories, the best resource is the *Stanford Encyclopedia of Philosophy* (http://www.plato.stanford.edu).

Surprisingly, humour can also help us to appreciate the essence of the philosophical theories which underlie bioethics. So, for light relief, you may want to read Cathcart and Klein's *Plato and a Platypus Walk into a Bar: Understanding Philosophy through Jokes* (2008).

PERSPECTIVES

In the first chapter I described moral theories as the 'heart' of bioethics. This is, of course, a metaphor, and metaphors can both illuminate and obscure our understanding. *Merely* following our heart can prevent us from noticing our prejudices, including our unquestioned ways of thinking. By describing bioethics in terms of different Western philosophical traditions, we may be missing important parts of the picture. So (to change the metaphor) we may need to alter the way we 'frame' bioethics in order to see it properly. What if our vision is distorted by our cultural assumptions? Or narrowed by our (unacknowledged) bias towards our own gender, be it male or female? Or blurred by our religious faith (or lack of it)? In this chapter I shall be describing a range of different perspectives on bioethics, in the hope of gaining a fuller picture of its richness and diversity. This is especially important when we realize that cultural diversity has become a global phenomenon and we need to learn to live with mutual understanding and respect between many different traditions and beliefs.

First, I shall look at a major influence on recent bioethics, feminist approaches, which seek to overcome the gender bias evident in health policies and in many discussions of bioethics issues. Next, I shall consider the contrast between cure and care in medicine, and take up the perspective of 'care ethics'. Lastly, I shall survey a wide range of viewpoints stemming from cultural differences in our globalized world and from the rich variety of religious belief.

GENDERED AGENDAS – FEMINIST APPROACHES

We start with feminist approaches to bioethics. There is no doubt that women, worldwide, carry a disproportionate burden of ill-health as well as an unequal share of caring for those who are ill or disabled. A recent report from the WHO (World Health Organization, 2009) showed that, although in higher-income countries women live longer than men, because of both biological and behavioural advantages, these advantages are outweighed, especially in lower-income countries, by gender discrimination, resulting in inequalities in education, income and employment and in access to health services. Moreover, the problems for women are especially severe in relation to sexuality and reproduction. The WHO report sums up the situation as follows:

> Globally, the leading cause of death among women of reproductive age is HIV/AIDS. Girls and women are particularly vulnerable to HIV infection due to a combination of biological factors and gender-based inequalities, particularly in cultures that limit women's knowledge about HIV and their ability to protect themselves and negotiate safer sex. The most important risk factors for death and disability in this age group in low- and middle-income countries are lack of contraception and unsafe sex. These result in unwanted pregnancies, unsafe abortions, complications of pregnancy and childbirth, and sexually transmitted infections including HIV. Violence is an additional significant risk to women's sexual and reproductive health and can also result in mental ill-health and other chronic health problems.
>
> (World Health Organization, 2009, p. xii)

Other major causes of injury and ill-health in women in poorer countries are burns from inadequate cooking facilities and respiratory problems from smoke inhalation. However, although gender discrimination is more severe in low- and middle-income countries, it is also a factor in wealthier countries, with consistent patterns of poorer access to health care and of an unequal share of care for elderly and disabled family members. Moreover, gender bias is also evident in medical research, with trials of medicines intended to be used by both sexes normally carried out only on male subjects. This policy has been adopted by pharmaceutical firms sponsoring trials in order to avoid the risk of administering a drug to women, who may (unknowingly) be pregnant. The Thalidomide scandal, in which many children were born with severe physical handicaps as a result of administration of this sleeping pill, which was thought also to help overcome morning sickness, had a major effect in entrenching this policy.

These stark instances of injustice based on gender alone provide the starting point for feminist approaches to bioethics. It is in essence a social and political critique of the way in which mainstream bioethics, wittingly or unwittingly, has bought into the gender bias of current institutions and practices in health care. This is not merely a matter of the failures of bioethical theory to give serious attention to issues of social justice: the feminist critique goes deeper than that, arguing that the whole manner of doing bioethics suffers from gender bias, that it is dominated by ways of thinking which are culturally masculine and has devalued alternative, more feminine ways of dealing with the issues it raises. In other words, bioethics not only prioritizes the issues that seem more important to men: it also seeks solutions in ways that men perceive as the correct approach.

At this point I need to stress that feminist scholars are not offering a different moral *theory* to rival the ones described in the previous chapter. There is, in fact, a range of different theories gathered under the banner of feminist approaches. Rather, we are being invited to shift our focus, or to reframe some of the questions we ask, so that we recognize the subtle ways in which the power imbalance between the sexes has affected all aspects of health and human welfare. We shall see this more clearly if we consider some of the key concepts in the feminist bioethics literature (and in feminist writing generally). These are: marginalization; embodiment; empowerment; and relational autonomy.

MARGINALIZATION

We saw in the WHO report that women's natural advantages in health and longevity have been eroded by cultural and social policies that fail to meet their needs or actively destroy their health. Much of this stems from sexist attitudes, which perceive women as inferior to men, physically, intellectually and even morally. Such misogynist classification of women regards them as naturally subservient to men, created to service male demands, yet, at the same time, dangerous sources of temptation and of irrationality. The Adam and Eve story in the Old Testament, in which it is Eve who listens to the serpent and then leads Adam astray, is a classic example of this disdain for women, but it finds ample expression today in policies which deny women basic human rights, such as education, the right to vote and equal opportunities and pay in employment. In its most extreme form this marginalization takes the form of physical abuse such as marital rape and 'female circumcision' (the surgical mutilation of the genitals of young girls to decrease their sexual pleasure, prevent intercourse prior to marriage, and increase the male's sensations from penetration).

Such oppression creates a sense of solidarity between feminist writers and those seeking justice for other marginalized groups, for example, the racially oppressed, the intellectually or physically disabled and the gay, lesbian and transgender community. In all these cases the mainstream (the explicit or implicit social norm of right behaviour) possesses the powerful current, sweeping all before it. At the margins of the stream are those who do not conform to the norm; left as flotsam at the edges, their worth is disregarded and their needs are ignored. Thus, feminist bioethics scholars see themselves, first and foremost, as advocates for those who are disempowered by gender discrimination. (They need not themselves be members of the marginalized group. Thus, some such writers are men.) To effect change many see the need to enter the mainstream of bioethics and try to influence the current, that is, the way in which the key issues are both defined and discussed. Thanks to these attempts to influence the mainstream of bioethics, the concepts I now discuss have gained greater prominence generally, though many mainstream authors still pay little attention to them.

EMBODIMENT

Feminist writers seek to re-assert the centrality of the body in bioethics, in opposition to the highly rationalistic focus of many theorists. Common stereotypes of masculine and feminine ways of grappling with moral issues portray men as rational, detached, with emotions in check, able to see the overarching moral issues which apply universally: women, on the contrary, are portrayed as emotional, over-involved, partial and limited in their ability to see the wider ramifications of their judgements I shall return to these alleged gender differences later, when discussing care ethics, but for the moment we need to see the danger of such a simplistic contrast. It reflects a philosophical approach known as Dualism, going back to the seventeenth-century philosopher René Descartes. This entails a radical split between mind and body (the philosopher of mind Gilbert Ryle describes this as seeing humans as 'ghosts in machines' (Ryle 1949)). In this view, the mind alone is capable of knowing the truth: the body is a mere container for the mind, and, because it is the source of feelings, it can be a distraction to clear thought.

We saw already in the previous chapter, when discussing Kant's theory, how such a radical split between reason and emotion can impoverish our account of ethics, leading to a cold, impersonal way of leading the moral life. Feminist writers have been active in trying to redress the balance by stressing the notion of 'embodiment'. Here we do not merely surrender to emotions, abandoning our capacity to reason, but we recognize that all of our experiences are mediated by our bodies, that our awareness of ourselves as unique individuals with a personal history is intimately connected to our body and its interactions with the environment. We are not free-floating, disembodied pools of consciousness. Without our body we literally would not know who we are, we would have no identity.

It may be that women, who have strong reminders of their bodily existence through menstruation, pregnancy, childbirth and breast feeding, are less likely to be caught up in this dualist fallacy than are men. But, for men and women alike, there is no getting away from our bodies. Some philosophers have viewed the body as a kind of prison from which we need to escape in order to be truly free. Instead, however, by recognizing and accepting our embodiment we may gain a greater freedom, as we shall see in the next section.

EMPOWERMENT

The marginalization discussed earlier often takes bodily form. The female body is seen as inferior to the male (and morally hazardous); equally, skin of the wrong colour can make one an outcast from birth; and less physically abled bodies (according to social norms of ability) are seen as housing less-worthy people. There also are many medical examples, both individual and social, of the body as a source of disgust, embarrassment or shame. The extreme cases of self-harm (cutting or burning one's body) and **anorexia** (starving the body, often with lethal effects) demonstrate how one's embodiment can become a source of self-hatred, particularly for young women. There are parallels in social attitudes. At one extreme, women are required by religious dogma to cover up the whole of their bodies, including their faces; at the other, women (and men also), enticed by the promises of cosmetic surgery to create a more attractive bodily image, have their bodies injected, excavated and surgically 'sculpted' in a quest for social success. These are all examples of disempowerment, though they may not all be perceived as such by those affected. The relationship between disempowerment and embodiment is especially clear for persons with physical disabilities. Because their bodies do not conform to the standard capacities of the majority in their society, they are prevented from achieving their full potential by an environment characterized by social exclusion and physical barriers.

Empowerment is achieved by breaking the vicious association between bodily form and moral or social worth. It entails a radical change in social attitudes and in the nature of the lived environment. But, equally, it entails an acceptance of one's embodiment, an affirmation of self-worth that includes one's specific bodily identity. Feminist thought has shown the way here, in its insistence that women can celebrate their biological nature, develop their own sources of power and authority, not be cowed into submission by the greater physical strength of men, and refuse to be treated as lesser beings, solely on account of their physical differences. These lessons from feminism have wide implications for all kinds of social discrimination, and push bioethics in the direction of a radical critique of our unquestioned assumptions in health and welfare policy.

RELATIONAL AUTONOMY

Another key feature of feminist thought is its rejection of individualism in ethics and its stress on the normative influence of social relationships. Here we can see links with the communitarian theory discussed in the last chapter. The feminist critique of oppressive social structures leads to a rejection of those accounts of autonomy which equate it with individual self-determination or the satisfaction of individual preferences. Such accounts fail to see that these ideals of individual choice are the privilege of those with power in society. Thus they are wholly inadequate for creating the conditions under which those who are discriminated against can genuinely find a means to fulfilment of their own valued choices.

The concept of 'relational autonomy' stresses our basic state of dependency, which sets limits to the extent to which we can escape the influence of family, culture and powerful social and political forces. Its goal, therefore, is to decrease the power of those social determinants that limit the development of individual capacities for fulfilling lives. For example, in patriarchal societies women may be prevented throughout their lives from taking any other role than that of home helper and carer of the older members of the family. Such women need supportive groups that can help them find the courage and means to live lives of greater richness and independence. The lone decider, exempt from social influence, is a philosopher's fantasy. But a supportive group can become the instrument for change to increased autonomy.

In summary, we can see that scholars of feminist approaches to bioethics try to change the way in which bioethical issues are framed. Whether it be gender discrimination or other forms of prejudice and injustice, they argue that we must not ignore the partly hidden social forces that influence the way we both describe and try to solve bioethical problems. We may still need a range of theory to structure our discussion and point to possible solutions, but this will be useful only if we are willing to initiate and sustain a radical critique of the institutions and professional practices that generate these problems. Feminist approaches to bioethics writing reminds us that we must always be open to the real possibility that we are asking the *wrong* questions!

TO CARE OR NOT TO CARE?

We saw in the previous section how, for feminists, the availability of supportive and empowering groups is an essential part of helping people to liberate themselves from oppressive social conditions. This leads us to consider a perspective on bioethics which puts the notion of 'care' at the centre of attention. To some extent this approach can be seen as a spin-off from feminism, since it also focuses on the centrality of relationships in ethics. The main exponent of the ethics of care, Nel Noddings, has described it as 'a *feminine* approach to ethics and moral education' (Noddings, 1984, my italics) – but here we see the hazard for feminism. We recall the stereotypes of masculinity and femininity, which feminism has fought against. This seems to play into the hands of those who want to promote gender-specific roles in health care: the (female) nurses do the caring, while the more rational and detached doctors (male, of course) do the curing! Such gender stereotypes are obviously nonsensical when we consider that in modern health care many men work as nurses and in many countries the majority of doctors are women, but they remain powerful stereotypes nonetheless.

Underlying Noddings' approach was some well-known research by Carol Gilligan (Gilligan 1982) which claimed to show that men and women reach moral decisions in different ways. For women, according to Gilligan's findings, commitment to specific personal relationships would be the deciding matter in ethical dilemmas; but for men the problem would be approached by reference to generalized moral principles. Thus, a feminine approach to ethics will always be very situational and case specific. (Given a different set of relationships, the moral choices could be quite different.) On the other hand, thinking in terms of universally applicable principles without altering them to fit cases is (according to this view) the masculine way of making decisions.

However, the Ethics of Care need not subscribe to these gendered distinctions. (In any case, Gilligan's research has since been seriously questioned.) Instead, we can see it as an approach which gives a new perspective on the moral theory of VE, described in the last chapter. What do we hope for when we speak of a 'virtuous' health care practitioner? Surely it is a mixture of these alleged masculine and feminine ways of making moral choices, in an appropriate balance (along the lines of Aristotle's golden mean). We certainly want practitioners to have the knowledge, intellect and skill to look objectively at our problem, and we do not want them to be so emotionally involved that they cannot help patients or see the medical issues clearly. Yet, at the same time, we do not want to be treated as 'a case', with no attention to ourselves as persons or to the unique circumstances in which our case arises. We also seek a sense of warmth, empathy and respect from those who help us when we are ill or dying, not merely a cold, clinical detachment.

This aspect of health care practice, the 'caring' aspect, has become increasingly important as the dramatic expansion of therapeutic interventions in modern health care has given the false idea that cure is always possible. This illusion (which is sometimes shared by both practitioners and patients) can result in everything short of total cure being seen as a failure, and so generate a *furor therapeuticus* (therapeutic frenzy), in which increasingly aggressive interventions are used in a futile attempt to avert death. Instead of this obsession with cure, health care practice needs to focus also on the skills of caring appropriately for the dying and for those with chronic illness. This is where the Ethics of Care perspective fits in. It can influence both the type of decision that is made and the way in which it is made. It can also guide the long-term relationship between patient and practitioner.

One way of describing this perspective is to make a distinction between 'caring for' and 'caring about' people. Both require a commitment to the other person, but there are subtle differences. Caring for can be quite physical and technical (a paradigm case would be the highly skilled nursing work involved in caring for patients in intensive care units); but 'caring about' is more personal and potentially more demanding on the health care practitioner. Beyond skill, it requires entering into the world of patients, knowing what matters to them and where their fears and hopes lie, sharing some of their pain, without being overwhelmed by it, and being a trusted companion on the journey they must make, whether to recovery or death. This aspect of health care can be the most rewarding part, but also the most difficult to sustain, and it is no surprise that 'burn out' is common in neonatal intensive care units (where the *parents* need such care), in paediatric oncology wards and in palliative care units. In all these cases, staff must try to find that Aristotelian mean between involvement and detachment, and it will be a difficult balance each time.

The Ethics of Care, then, is clearly an important perspective for bioethics, but it is not in any sense a moral theory, which helps to give the answers in difficult decisions. Instead it may provide some help to the decision maker as these decisions become painful and burdensome. It describes an attitude, a habit of the heart, which both men and women need if they choose to work in situations where others are experiencing deep suffering and loss.

CULTURE AND RELIGION

Another set of perspectives comes in when we consider the influence of culture and religion on ethics. To what extent can we speak of a universal or global bioethics? We now turn to this question, already referred to when we discussed VE and feminist approaches to bioethics. No one could doubt that our moral beliefs and decision making are influenced by our upbringing in a specific cultural context; and that this will include, for many people, the beliefs and practices of a religious tradition. But how normative should these influences be? Should we suppose that each of us is *trapped* in our own culture and belief system, so that there is no possibility of a shared human morality? The view that this is the case is called ethical relativism, and it claims that any kind of appeal to a universal moral law is illusory (and most likely just a hidden way of imposing the beliefs of one culture on others). For example, the human rights movement has been seen by some Asian writers and politicians as a form of cultural imperialism – the imposition of a set of Western liberal values on Eastern societies, which operate in a more hierarchical, authoritarian manner based on tradition.

But there are serious problems with ethical relativism. The first is a philosophical puzzle: if all beliefs are purely relative in this way, then isn't the belief that all beliefs are relative also relative? If this is so, how can we say that ethical relativism is universally true? Maybe it is only true for the person claiming it, but for others ethical universalism could be equally true. (This puzzle is reminiscent of an ancient logical conundrum: You meet a man on the road, who says, 'All Cretans are liars, and I am a Cretan'. Is he telling the truth? If he is telling the truth, then he is a Cretan – and so he is not telling the truth!)

A more practical objection to ethical relativism is that there are some cases in which we simply cannot accept its conclusions. A strong example of this is the genital mutilation of young girls referred to earlier, a practice supported by the mothers of the girls in some cultures because they fear that their daughters will not be able to marry if it is not carried out. Yet most societies have outlawed this practice. Is this culturally insensitive? Cultural imperialism? Surely it is better described as defending the right of these girls to be protected from such terrible harm. (Yet the social conditions leading to such harms are also very difficult to overcome. For example, in countries where rape of young girls is common, mothers have been known to burn the faces and breasts of their daughters, in the hope that they will be less attractive to the rapists. This again is surely wrong, but rendering the society a safe place for young women may take years.) Another example of the moral unacceptability of relativism can be taken from racial discrimination. Was apartheid morally acceptable because it was the moral belief of one cultural group in South Africa? Again, this does not seem to be a morally relative matter. To recognize the civil and political rights of all persons, whatever the colour of their skin, is surely a universal moral value.

For these reasons, it seems better to talk about cultural *influences* as significant aspects of morality, but not to accept that they are so utterly determinative of it that there is no point in seeking universal human values. In the field of bioethics, debate about these different cultural factors has focused mainly on the alleged differences in Eastern and Western ways of seeking solutions to bioethical problems. In short, is there an 'Asian Bioethics' which is significantly different from the dominant theories of ethics coming from Western Europe and the USA? I shall briefly consider this claim next.

EAST MEETS WEST

Asia covers an immense land mass which contains five of the seven most populous nations in the world and its population is

60 per cent of the world's total. All the major world religions originated in Asia: Hinduism, Buddhism, Judaism, Christianity and Islam. It also has a widespread practice of traditional medicine, especially in China and other countries with large Chinese populations (Traditional Chinese Medicine) and in the Indian subcontinent (Ayurvedic Medicine). At the same time, the globalization of trade and the rapid spread of mass communications have brought dramatic changes to the traditional cultures, and put several Asian nations in the forefront of economic growth. Western medicine is also very highly developed in Asia, and many countries have succeeded in being 'medical tourist hubs', with the quality, but lower cost, of medical and surgical practice attracting patients from all over the world (often at the cost of an adequate health care system for the country's own inhabitants, since the provision of private medical care starves the public services of funds and personnel).

Given the sheer, size, diversity and rapid evolution of Asia, it is hard to imagine what could be called distinctively 'Asian' bioethics. Nevertheless, attempts have been made to do this. Usually a contrast is drawn with Western bioethics, with its stress on individual autonomy, individual rights and justice gained through contract and negotiation. Asian bioethics, on the other hand, has been said to be based on social harmony, reflected in an ordered society, the pre-eminence of the duties rather than the rights of individuals and the subordination of individual preference to the welfare of the family or the society as a whole. This account of Asian bioethics can be summed up as 'familial communitarianism'.

However, this stark contrast between Western and Eastern values seems like a gross simplification. We already saw that an over-emphasis on individual autonomy has been criticized by many Western theorists, including feminist writers and communitarians. Equally, Kantian ethics has a stress on duty as much as on rights, and VE promotes harmony and balance. Moreover, Asian writers have warned of the dangers of an overstress on social order, which leads easily to patriarchy in the home and in the medical setting, and the suppression of dissent in civil society. A better approach may be to see that *some* of the traditional values of Asian societies can help to ensure a balanced view of the place of the individual in the society. Such an exercise can benefit both East and West.

We can illustrate this approach to the potentially beneficial influence of culture by looking in more detail at one of the powerful philosophical and social influences in many parts of Asia: Confucianism. This is an ancient philosophy originating in China and going back over two-and-a-half millennia, yet it is still actively studied and applied today. One of its distinctive features is that it is not a moral *theory*, designed to solve dilemmas. (But it is not normally described as a religion either.) Rather it concerns the *practice* of *ren*, which can be translated narrowly to refer to the particular virtue of benevolence, and more broadly to refer to an ethical orientation that encompasses and guides all other virtues. Fan, a proponent of 'Confucian bioethics', describes Confucianism as follows:

> Confucian morality is embedded in a way of life directed towards virtue and sustained by rituals or rites (*li*). The focus is not primarily on resolving controversial cases, but instead on understanding properly what it is to live as a virtuous human.
>
> (Fan, 2012)

We can see obvious connections with VE here, but what is distinctive is the emphasis on *li* or rites or rituals, which have ethical, aesthetic and religious dimensions and are regarded as vital to the expression of our emotions, values and attitudes towards virtuous conduct (see Cua, 2002). Many rites are directed towards the family, for example, funeral rites. Others deal with relationships with others, for example, greeting rituals. Like other social norms, ritual traditions can be adapted or departed from, if appropriate, in response to changing contexts. From a Confucian perspective, what is important is having or developing the right ethical spirit in ritual participation (Chong, 1999); both spirit and form are necessary for the cultivation of human personhood and the ordering of human relations towards meaning and the flourishing life.

This ancient teaching provides another – perhaps unexpected – perspective on bioethics. It provides insights into how individuals and families might face up to some of the insoluble and inescapable ordeals of injury and illness by appealing to the wisdom of the past and to the power of ritual. In later chapters we shall see this perspective illuminating some of the specific dilemmas of bioethics, but, for now, it serves as a link to the next section of this chapter: the place of religion in bioethics.

RELIGION AND BIOETHICS

According to the psychoanalyst Erich Fromm, religion offers two things to the believer: 'a frame of orientation and an object of devotion' (Fromm, 1950). If we apply this to bioethics, we can see two possibilities for the relevance of religion. Firstly, it may offer a different way of viewing the dilemmas and suggest different solutions from those coming from secular moral theory; secondly, though it may not affect the *content* of the values held and the decisions made, it may provide the *motivation* to act morally. (This second feature, motivation coming from an object of devotion, is summed up in the Christian tradition by what Jesus called the greatest commandment: 'You shall love the Lord your God with all your heart and with all your soul and with all your strength and with all your mind, and your neighbour as yourself' (Luke 10:27, English Standard Version).)

We shall now look briefly at five major world religions, some of which are more directly concerned with the content of ethics (as well as encouraging the moral life), whilst others are more focused on devotional practices and obedience to a way of life than on specific ethical requirements.

But first, we need to clarify how, if at all, religion can be of relevance to bioethics, except in the restricted sense that it matters to those who believe in it and practice it. What place does religion have in our modern, pluralistic societies, many of which have a very small percentage of believers? Is there any place for religious perspectives in secular civic society? There are two problems here: the first relates to the relationship of religious teaching to the values of bioethics; the second relates to the claim that religion motivates people to act rightly.

The first problem goes back to a discussion in one of Plato's dialogues (the *Euthyphro*), in which Socrates asks the question: Is something good because God wills it; or does God will it because it is good? So, when people say that they are doing (or not doing) something because 'it is the will of God', what is added by them saying that it is God's will? Do they mean that only believers can know what is the right thing to do? Or do they mean that they will always do whatever God commands, since faith trumps morality, *even if* they (or others) see it as wrong? (A classic example of this second approach is the story in the Old Testament in which God tests Abraham's faith by telling him to kill his son Isaac (Genesis 22, English Standard Version).) Most people, including many religious believers, would not agree with *either* of these claims, however. They would not accept that you have to be religious in order to know what is right, and they would not want to believe in a God who commanded you to do something morally wrong, like sacrificing an innocent child. So they would have to accept the second horn of Plato's dilemma: God's will is always in conformity with what is good. But this then seems to make religion redundant in ethics, since goodness or rightness can be established independently of God. I shall return to this dilemma when I survey those religious traditions which make claims to provide special insights into moral questions in bioethics (and in ethics in general). But, for the moment, I have classed religions as 'perspectives' rather than moral theories, because I see their contribution to bioethics as being different from providing generally applicable solutions to ethical problems.

But now we come to the second problem. What about religion being seen as a source of inspiration to act morally? As we shall see, most religions do exhort believers to live good lives, and many provide practical guidance on how to achieve this. Moreover, there are many historical examples of ways in which religious belief has motivated people to provide help for the sick and the needy, to seek justice for those suffering from social neglect and discrimination, and to work for peace and reconciliation in times of conflict. But, on the other hand, religion can also have a powerfully malign effect, provoking and supporting lethal violence in the name of some allegedly religious cause. From the Christian Crusades in the Middle Ages to the terrorist attacks and suicide bombers of the present era there are many examples of so-called 'holy wars'. It seems, then, that while religious belief can be a strong motivational factor, it is not always on the side of the welfare of all humanity. It may be a healing and uniting influence, but it can also provoke fear, hatred and violent strife. The deep feelings it engenders are not always ones that lead to respect, compassion and care for the other, whoever they are. This means that the relationship between religion and bioethics will always be somewhat ambiguous.

In the subsections which follow I shall now give a brief overview of five religious traditions as these relate to bioethics. There are of course many more than five religions in the world, but I have chosen these because of their extensive influence globally. However, a note of caution is needed here. Firstly, these short summaries cannot possibly do justice to such rich traditions, and readers should follow up with the readings at the end of this chapter if this is an interest of theirs. Secondly, all the traditions are complex and diverse, with significant internal differences. This means that we have to avoid suggesting that there is, for example, *one* Christian, or Islamic, or Buddhist view on particular issues in bioethics. I have tried to avoid these over-simplifications by staying at a general level, conveying the main features of the tradition, rather than going to the level of specific judgements on the ethical issues. Finally, it should be noted that I am not giving priority to any religious tradition, and for this reason I am surveying them in historical order, looking first at two major religious traditions originating in South Asia (Hinduism and Buddhism) and then at three 'Abrahamic' religions, Judaism, Christianity and Islam (the latter two being developments from the first).

THE WAYS OF DHARMA: HINDUISM AND BUDDHISM

In surveying two ancient religious traditions originating in the Indian subcontinent, Hinduism and Buddhism, we must first realize that the modern Western way of seeing religion, ethics and culture as separate spheres simply does not fit the way in which these traditions operate. The religious practices described in the West as 'Hinduism' or 'Buddhism' (these are not labels which those practising them would comfortably apply themselves) do not fit well into the Western notion of a 'religious faith' as being a central set of beliefs and ethical requirements. Instead, we need to see what I have called the 'way of *dharma*' as the governing feature, where the word dharma refers to a universal spirituality which maintains and nurtures all life. The original form of this spirituality is *sanatana dharma* ('immemorial dharma') or Hindu-*dharma* – what is called in the West 'Hinduism'. From this 'mother' there have come 'daughters' – Buddha-*dharma*, Jaina-*dharma* and Sikh-*dharma* – Buddhism, Jainism and Sikhism. (Notably, Hindus consider the three 'Abrahamic' religions – Judaism, Christianity and Islam – also as ways of *dharma*.) In all of the *dharmic* traditions, social practices, cultural norms, ethical requirements, beliefs and religious rituals are inextricably woven together. I shall be summarizing just two of them – Hinduism and Buddhism – but, in all four, the concept of some kind of distinctive and separate ethical perspective is somewhat alien. Instead, they advocate and sustain a way of living and being – how to live, rather than what to believe or how to know what is right.

HINDUISM

As the oldest of the religious traditions, Hinduism has evolved in a vast variety of forms, finding different expression across a wide range of cultures and ethnic groups, largely, though not exclusively, in the Indian subcontinent. There are at least six different schools of Hindu philosophical systems, with many more on the fringes of orthodoxy. Still more diversity comes from a central feature of this approach, that it accepts all religious beliefs and practices as equally valid ways for the enlightenment of the soul; concepts of atheism, heresy and orthodoxy do not make much sense in this openness to all spirituality; and proselytization to a particular religious faith is quite alien to it. Interestingly, founders of other religious faith traditions – Buddha, Christ or Muhammad – are considered as *avataras* (prophets) like Krishna in the Hindu faith tradition.

Given such openness and diversity, any attempt to summarize the main features of Hinduism has to be tentative and provisional. Nevertheless, we can point to some common elements, which give its adherents a distinctive way of understanding, and dealing with, the issues of bioethics. As we saw in our earlier discussion of common features of bioethics in Asia, Hinduism focuses on *kartabya* (duties), rather than on individual rights. These duties enter into all aspects of daily life and its course over the years, including performing the right rituals at birth and death, fulfilling family obligations, especially in the care of children and of the elderly, and performing one's designated role in the family (for example, as the eldest son) and in the wider society. A second main feature of Hinduism is its emphasis on achieving harmony in both human life and the environment as a whole. The principle of *ahimsa* (the avoidance of all forms of harm) means that one must constantly strive to preserve the integrity and sanctity of life in all its forms and to rectify imbalances in nature. From this come the practice of avoiding killing unnecessarily even the lowliest forms of life, and various forms of dietary practice, including full or partial vegetarianism. Third, Hinduism emphasizes purity and purification of mind, body and spirit. Its daily rituals and other religious practices, for example, taking a holy dip in the Ganges, are aimed at overcoming the contamination which is an inevitable part of earthly life and at helping the eternal spirit present in each person (the *atman*) to be freed from the cycles of birth and death and to achieve its liberation *(moksha)*.

However, we must avoid seeing only the externals of Hindu practice in rituals, social arrangements and temple worship. In at least some of its forms, Hindu belief encourages and sustains a deep personal spirituality. Perhaps the most recognizable form is the idea that *Atman* is *Brahman* (the *self* is one with the *divine*). Not all forms of Hinduism share this precept in the same way, as there are dualistic *(dvaita)* and non-dualist *(advaita)* forms, and the above is *advaita*. However, *advaita Vedanta* was the form that first came to the West, and is one of the major philosophical traditions in modern Hinduism. The basic idea is that each of us is 'one with the divine', although we do not fully realize it, and the purpose of religious practice is to remove this ignorance in order to recognize our oneness. And *Guru* is the guide who leads one from the darkness of ignorance to the light of knowledge. Thus, morality flows from treating each other (and all elements of the universe – animate and inanimate) as part of our (or the) *one* Self. Practices (to arrive at this deep-seated knowing) vary widely from the intellectual *(jnani)* to the devotional *(bhakti)* and include physical approaches (parts of yoga) and service *(seva)* – or work without expectation of reward. These practices, sustained over many lifetimes of birth and rebirth, lead inevitably to enlightenment or *samadh*.

Hinduism thus does not aim directly at morality, rather, 'moral' precepts aid living in a balanced harmonious way in order to know our true nature (being 'one with the divine') or achieve emancipation *(mukti)*. So, if we understand our true nature or creation (manifestation of God), we do not behave immorally, as that would be to harm the (same) divinity in another person that they share with me. Thus, unlike in the 'Abrahamic' traditions stemming from Judaism, there is no 'original sin', no Fall (the exclusion from paradise caused by our sinfulness). Our major blemish is ignorance of our true nature – or not following the way of *dharma*.

BUDDHISM

I noted earlier that there are four forms of *dharma*, of which Hinduism is the earliest. In terms of world religions with widespread influence, Buddhism is the only other *dharma* to be considered in this very brief survey. It originated in India in the fifth century BCE with the teachings of the historical figure Siddhartha Gautama. Although he was given the honorific title 'the Buddha', this is not a proper name but a description, meaning 'Awakened One' or 'Enlightened One'. Buddhist tradition recognizes the possibility of many other 'buddhas', and Siddhartha himself is regarded as an entirely human person (not in any sense divine, as Jesus of Nazareth was claimed to be in the Christian tradition). Over the nearly two-and-a-half thousand years of its existence Buddhism has developed a large body of teachings (known as *Dharma*) and has spread throughout Asia, and more recently also in the West. It has two main traditions (but also derivatives from these): the Theravada school, which is the con-servative guardian of the ancient tradition going back to the first scriptures, known as the Pali Canon; and the more innovative Mahayana movement, from which both Tibetan Buddhism and Zen Buddhism are derived. The former school is the dominant one in South-East Asia and Sri Lanka, whilst variations of the Mahayana approach are found in North and East Asia.

Despite these historical and geographical differences, however, scholars have identified some common central features of Buddhist teaching that are of relevance to ethics. These are: rebirth, *karma* and the Four Noble Truths. Whilst Hinduism and Buddhism share similar beliefs about rebirth and *karma*, the emphasis given to these beliefs in Buddhism sets it very clearly apart from the dominant religions in the West, where the focus is on the *one* life led by an *individual self*. In Buddhism my present life is merely one in a succession of countless lives, taking different forms (including many non-human forms) and stretching back into a forgotten past. Moreover, ahead of this life there is the potential for many more rebirths in different forms. Thus, the notion of 'my personal life' is an illusion, which I must eventually discard in order to achieve *Nirvana*, a timeless state that transcends all other forms of existence.

Just what form each of my lives takes is determined by my *karma*. This is often translated as my 'fate', but the concept of karma is subtler than simple fatalism, which sees my future as wholly predetermined, rendering my current 'choices' totally irrelevant. According to karma, my present actions will determine both my happiness in this life and my future life, so if I lead a life of hatred, violence or lust, the nature of my next life will reflect this, in the form of the being I become. On the other hand, though I may have developed a bad character in previous lives, and so risk actions that will lead to a bad karma, I can overcome this, live a virtuous life and so make choices that will affect my future destiny; and perhaps, finally, after countless years and lives, I may achieve Nirvana.

The Four Noble Truths spell out in more detail this account of our destiny. The first truth is that life as we know it is inherently unsatisfactory and inevitably leads to suffering of many kinds. The second truth is that the source of this unsatisfactory life is that we are in the grip of insatiable desires or cravings, which will always make our lives ones of constant dissatisfaction and frustration. The third truth is that we can escape from this cycle of suffering and frustration only by detaching ourselves from these pointless selfish desires and attachments; thereby, we may escape the turning wheel of existence (*samsara*) with its countless rebirths, and perhaps even achieve the state of Nirvana at the end of our earthly life. The fourth truth is that we will attain this perfection by following the 'middle way', which means observing the guidance for living called the Eightfold Path. There are two forms of this Path, the ordinary and the Noble. Following the ordinary version can lead to good karma and so to a better rebirth. For a few, the higher, Noble Path provides preparation for attaining Nirvana.

In this short summary, I cannot describe all the detail of the Path. (The reading list at the end of the chapter gives helpful sources for this.) In brief, the Path covers three aspects of right living: developing moral virtue; meditation; and attaining wisdom. An often-quoted verse from the traditional writings in the Pali Canon summarizes this approach:

> Not to do any evil,
> to cultivate what is wholesome,
> to purify one's mind:
> this is the teaching of the Buddhas
>
> (Roebuck, 2010, *The Dhammapada*, verse 183)

RELEVANCE TO BIOETHICS

As I observed earlier, there is a real danger that a brief summary like the one I have just given will fail to do justice to the richness and diversity of the religious traditions described in this section. But perhaps I have conveyed something of the tone of both Hindu and Buddhist ethics. In some respects they are reminiscent of the VE theories described in the previous chapter, since they focus on the development of goodness in the individual within a social setting. However, rather than simply moral development, both these traditions see spiritual development and liberation from both ignorance and desire as the ultimate goal. As byproducts of this (or – perhaps better – as integral to this spiritual development) there come care and compassion for all forms of life, and a cultivation of the self that weeds out selfish desires and attitudes of disrespect, envy or hatred toward others. Thus, the pursuit of virtue is one part of the way to human fulfilment. Yet, in other respects these forms of spirituality are somewhat different from the kind of VE espoused by Aristotle and his modern followers. For Aristotle the goal of *eudaimonia* was to be reached through the right exercise of our given human nature, a fulfilment in this life. But for Hinduism and Buddhism any particular lifetime and the individual that lives it become of importance only because of the part of the journey – in this life – toward *moksha* or *Nirvana*. So one should live one's earthly life with non-attachment, recognizing that everything is impermanent. All life, be it human or non-human, is one, a single stream, in which our individuality has only relative meaning.

Thus, the distinctiveness of the Buddhist and Hindu approaches to bioethics is not obviously related to the detailed dilemmas of decision making in health care. We might deduce some specific guidance on life-and-death issues, such as abortion or euthanasia, from the high valuation of all life, but the connections are not always very strong. Of greater relevance is the meditative detachment which they teach, giving a whole new perspective from which to view the threats and suffering of illness and death. Equally, the sense of organic unity with all things around us, which comes when we cease to be caught in the greedy exploitation of the earth's resources that is evident in most human activity, has much to say to that aspect of bioethics which is concerned with environmental neglect and destruction. There is no 'ethical theory' (in the Western sense of that term) here: but there could be a new way of finding wisdom and tranquillity, as well as a deep care and compassion for all who suffer.

THE 'ABRAHAMIC' RELIGIONS

The other main family of world religions originates with the monotheistic faith of the Hebrew patriarch Abraham, as portrayed in the Hebrew Scriptures. Although in many ways very different from each other, these three religions share a common emphasis on orthodoxy of belief (in one God) and on detailed guidance on ethical behaviour.

JUDAISM

Dating back for at least three-and-a-half thousand years, Judaism is the first of these three religions. It takes as its authoritative source the Hebrew Scriptures (called 'the Old Testament' by Christians and 'the Hebrew Bible' or 'Tanakh' by Jews — Tanakh is an acronym of Torah (teaching), Nevim (prophets) and Ketuvim (writings)). The first five books of these scriptures (the Torah) contain the fundamental teachings of Judaism. They describe how God made an agreement (a 'covenant') with the people of Israel, identifying them as his specially chosen people, who were entrusted to set an example of holiness and ethical behaviour to all humankind. These scriptures also contain the Ten Commandments and a long list of detailed laws and ritual requirements, including dietary restrictions and required modes of dress and appearance. An orthodox Jew will believe that these laws must be followed to the letter, since they are direct commandments from God, conveyed to the Jewish people through Moses.

It can be seen, then, that Judaism, at least in its strictly orthodox form, is basically ethnocentric – only a person born of a Jewish mother can be one of the chosen people, and, if born a Jew, one cannot cease to be one, even if one stops believing in or practising the faith. This strong sense of ethnic identity is further reinforced (again in orthodox practice) by an emphasis on the family as a place of remembrance of Jewish history in the Passover meal (*seder*), by strict observance of the Sabbath as a day of rest and meditation only, by worship in the synagogue and special rituals associated with birth, coming of age, marriage and death, and by the longing to return to the holy place, Mount Zion in Jerusalem, the location of the Jewish Temple until its destruction by the Romans in 70 CE. Over the centuries since that catastrophic event, this sense of uniqueness and of a special identity has been maintained by many Jews, despite their being scattered over numerous countries (what is known as the Jewish Diaspora) and being frequently discriminated against and violently persecuted, most recently in the Nazi Holocaust.

However, this sense of uniqueness as a people should not be seen as some claim to racial superiority: on the contrary, in its purest form it is more a sense of responsibility to live exemplary lives and an awareness of the repeated failure to do what God wishes them to do in the world. This sense of betrayal of the covenant with God and of repeated challenge to do better in the future is a constant theme both in the Torah and in the Hebrew prophets. As a result, there is a powerfully humane strand in Jewish belief and practice, leading to major involvement in medicine and the caring professions as a whole, as well as in international movements for justice and humanitarian aid. For many Jews, justice is the core ethical value in Judaism, and this has been expressed in the Hebrew phrase *tikkun olam* ('repairing the world') – a God-given mission to which Jews must remain faithful.

When it comes to law and ethics, there is a strong emphasis on deriving judgements from the scholarly interpretation of documents like the Torah and other Jewish scriptures, and from the Talmud (a record of scholarly interpretations of the Jewish law over many centuries by recognized teachers (rabbis)), and on attempting to relate these to contemporary issues, even although the historic documents may have little or nothing to say directly about them. This way of approaching ethics in Jewish tradition is summed up by the term *Halakhah*, which might best be translated as 'walking the right path', as required by the Jewish law. Guidance will be given by Jewish scholars in the form of *responsa*, judgements on how Jews should respond to contemporary issues which are not explicitly dealt with in the traditional sources of guidance.

However, an emphasis on legalistic interpretation will fail to do justice to the diversity of approaches within the Jewish religious community. Since the nineteenth century there have been numerous reform movements in Judaism, seeking to relate it more effectively to contemporary life and practice. There is a range of different groups, but the three main divisions are between Orthodox Judaism, Conservative Judaism and Reform Judaism. As the name implies, the Orthodox groups (which include Modern Orthodox, ultra-Orthodox and Hasidism) require strict adherence to the Jewish Law and see all of it as divinely inspired and literally true. This means, for example, the segregation of the sexes in the synagogue, strict adherence to dietary requirements and an uncompromising approach to such issues as abortion, euthanasia and homosexuality. The Reform movement, on the other hand, sees the Law as important but not the final arbiter on moral issues. This results in equality of the sexes in worship and practice, including allowing women to be rabbis, and more liberal attitudes toward bioethical issues relating to life, death and sexuality. The Conservative group occupies a middle position between these two groups, seeing the Law as the fundamental guide for Jews, but allowing for flexibility in interpreting it. Like the Reform movement, it opposes scriptural fundamentalism and allows far more scope for human reason. However, it is more traditional in its worship and ritual practices (though not insisting on segregation of the sexes). On ethical issues, Conservative Jews are likely to be more open to toleration of what would be unacceptable to Orthodox Jews, for example, the acceptance of gays in the community, including in positions of religious leadership.

Given this diversity within the same religious tradition, we are left wondering what specific perspective on bioethics is to be found in the religion as a whole. There is no *one* Jewish ethical position, any more than there is one Christian or Islamic one (as we shall see later). However, like the other Abrahamic religions, Judaism has a powerfully prophetic stance: it is never merely a matter of personal piety or of some sort of individualistic cultivation of the soul. All its rituals are directed towards the sustaining of family life, but also towards strengthening the community and preparing it for its role in the world outside the religious group. To be a Covenanted People means to have duties toward humanity as a whole. This means that a Jewish perspective on bioethics can never rest content with issues of personal autonomy and rights: it will always raise questions about justice, and about the treatment of the most neglected and maltreated of our fellow humans. (In theory at least, those who have known such persecution in their history must surely always see themselves on the side of the oppressed.) Thus, the Jewish perspective provides a powerful commitment to combating all forms of injustice in the world, including those evident in health care.

CHRISTIANITY

Of all the five religions to be summarized and discussed, Christianity is arguably the most complex and diverse. Starting out as a small Jewish sect in the first century CE, it grew, spread and split into numerous groups, to become the largest of all the world religions and also one of the most influential in the development of modern culture, especially in the West. Despite the increased secularization of Western societies in the twentieth and twenty-first centuries, Christianity is still powerfully associated with Western cultural values, especially in the USA.

However, Christianity has also had a long history of disagreement over doctrine leading to massive splits, first, that which separated the Eastern (Orthodox) Church from the Western (Roman) Church in the eleventh century, and then the Protestant Reformation beginning in the fifteenth century, leading not only to a departure from the Roman Catholic Church by Protestants, but also to the subsequent fragmentation of Protestants into numerous smaller denominations. For this reason, the idea that there can be *the* Christian view on any issue is clearly mistaken.

Nevertheless, despite all this diversity and disagreement, Christians do hold a number of beliefs in common. Firstly, they derive from their Jewish heritage a belief in one God (monotheism) and they regard the Old Testament as one source of authority for them. (Thus, for example, the title given to Jesus, the 'Christ' or the 'Messiah' – meaning 'the Anointed One' – is seen by Christians as a fulfilment of a prophecy in the Old Testament, as is the belief that Jesus's mother was a virgin.) But, secondly, Christians depart from Judaism in their belief that Jesus of Nazareth was the incarnation of God, or the son of God, and that, although he was executed by the Romans, he rose from the dead and joined God the Father in heaven, sending the Holy Spirit to continue to guide his followers. This belief in one God, but revealed in three persons, is known as the Doctrine of the Trinity and is a distinctive feature of most (but not all) Christian groups. Thirdly, the scriptures written after the death of Jesus, known collectively as the New Testament, are the most authoritative source of guidance about both belief and behaviour for Christians, and subsequent doctrine is tested by reference to them. However, interpretation of both the Old and the New Testaments has varied hugely over the centuries, and only some Christians (known as Biblical Fundamentalists) believe in the literal truth of everything that is written in them.

When we consider ethics in general, and modern bioethics in particular, we can see that Christianity has had (at least until very recently) a major influence. We can see two sources here. The first is the teaching of Jesus, as reported in the New Testament, that every person is of infinite worth in the eyes of God, that God is especially concerned with the needs of the poor, the outcast and the sick, and that our fundamental way of honouring and loving God is to love our neighbours as ourselves. This command to love was seen as greater than any of the detailed requirements of the Jewish Law, and one which applied to all humans, whatever their origin or beliefs. The parable of the Good Samaritan summed all this up. The Samaritans and the Judeans despised one another, and therefore the idea of a 'good' Samaritan, who would stop to help a Jew lying injured at the side of the road, would have been a startling example in the first century CE. This teaching should have had radical implications for both personal and social life, but in fact the institutionalization of Christianity, first in the Roman Empire and then for centuries later in the 'Christian' countries of the West, meant that racism, social inequality (including its extreme form, slavery) and disregard for the poor and oppressed were rarely questioned, except by a minority of Christians. Yet, when it is not obscured by the appropriation of religion by the powerful, this approach to ethics is in total harmony with the goals of medicine and can provide it with the core values that we seek from health care providers, such as caring for all who are sick, irrespective of their beliefs or their social standing.

In addition to this fundamental commitment to an ethics of non-discriminatory love of the neighbour, the Christian tradition has developed very detailed ethical guidance, based partly, but not exclusively, on biblical sources. Here, a powerful influence came from the mediaeval theologian Thomas Aquinas. He combined Christian teaching with the philosophy of Aristotle and of sub-sequent classical writers, and sought to discern the Natural Law, the set of moral rules that all humans could recognize and through which they would find fulfilment of their natures. The incorpora-tion of Natural Law into Christian teaching meant that the ethical demands were not restricted to believers, but would apply equally to all humans. We shall see later how this aspect of Christian ethics has had a profound effect on debates in bioethics, especially in the field of reproductive medicine. But, for the present, we can simply note a tension in the Christian perspectives on bioethical issues. On the one hand, it can push for an open and caring attitude to all the dilemmas that we encounter in this field; on the other, it can endorse (whether from a rigid interpretation of Natural Law or from a fundamentalist reading of biblical texts) a narrow and legalistic approach to bioethics. One thing is clear: whether we are discussing the beginning or the end of life, there will never be *one* Christian view of the right thing to do.

ISLAM

The religion known as 'Islam' (which means 'voluntary submission to God') began in the seventh century CE with the prophet Muhammad (born in 570 CE). Muslims regard him as the last and the greatest of a line of prophets that includes Abraham, Moses and Jesus. The revelations to Muhammad, subsequently written in the Qur'an, are regarded as the literal word of God, correcting the distortions of Judaism and Christianity. Together with the Sunna (the teachings of Muhammad and normative examples taken from his life), the Qur'an forms the absolute authority for all Islamic belief and practice. Despite this common basis, however, Islam has split over the centuries into five different schools of scholars interpreting the application of the basic texts. Four of these schools come under the largest denomination in Islam, the Sunni, and the fifth school, the Shi'i, under the Shi'a denomination (comprising about 10 to 20 per cent of Muslims worldwide, but over 80 per cent in Iran).

Given the diversity of scholarship, and the absence of any central authority in Islam (unlike the church authorities in some Christian denominations), it is not possible to describe a single Islamic position on most ethical issues, including those in bioethics. Instead there is a range of scholarly interpretations of the application of God's law to specific situations, leading to a body of Shari'a Law, which may apply in one situation, but then can be open to question by subsequent scholarly interpretation of the tradition or by scholars in another school of thought in Islam.

There is, however, a set of core beliefs, common to all Muslims, known as the Five Pillars. These apply primarily to religious belief and practice. They are: (1) Testimony ('There is only one God and Muhammad is his messenger'); (2) Prayer (to be observed five times daily); (3) Fasting (from dawn to dusk in the month of Ramadan); (4) Almsgiving (*Zakaat*, a set proportion of one's income given to charity and to aid the spread of Islam); and (5) Pilgrimage (at least once in a lifetime to make the *Hajj* to Mecca). If one wanted to convey the spirit of Islam, it is to be found in the meaning of the term itself, 'voluntary submission to the will of God'. Thus, religious discipline and a constant attempt to do God's will are characteristic of the religion, despite its plurality of forms of belief and practice.

What, then, might this mean for bioethics? Many readers of this book may confuse Islamic ethics with the religious fundamentalism of the Taliban and other extremist political and religious groups. Thus, the individual interpretation and the barbaric punishments of some applications of Shari'a Law and the repression of women through enforced marriages, insistence on the total body covering of the burqa, denial of educational and employment opportunity and unequal marital rights are often seen to be typical of Islamic ethics. But this is to ignore the centuries of scholarship going back to the Middle Ages which has shaped and enriched the Islamic view of medicine, the sciences and ethical judgements. It is also to ignore the moderation and flexibility of contemporary Islamic bioethics scholars and of the vast majority of Muslim believers. Rather than a repressive dogmatism, most Islamic judgements try to reconcile the tradition with the new demands of modern society and to seek an alliance between religion, technology and scientific innovation.

Perhaps the most characteristic feature of Islamic bioethics is that it is *jurisprudential*, which means that it relies on scholarly directives (*fatwa*) on specific questions raised, rather than on broad and overarching ethical principles. This set of religious/legal judgements (known as *fiqh*) will be based on several sources: firstly, the words of the Qur'an; secondly, the traditional religious judgements of the earliest era (the Sunna); thirdly, a search for a consensus among established Islamic religious authorities; and finally, the use of reason. The wide variation in Islamic judgements on specific bioethical issues, such as abortion, cloning, assisted reproduction and the use of genetic information, can be explained by the interpretation and different emphasis placed on these four routes to judgement listed above. For some scholars, literal textual quotations may bulk large, whilst for others reason will play a much larger part. (In this respect, however, Islam is really no different from the other 'Abrahamic' religions, Christianity and Judaism, both of which encompass a wide range from textual fundamentalism to a broadly liberal and rationalist approach to ethics; and the tradition of *fiqh* has great similarities to the Jewish tradition of *responsa* described earlier.)

As a perspective on bioethics, Islam is clearly important for two reasons. Firstly, it represents the second-largest – and rapidly growing – group of religious believers worldwide, whose daily life and practice are strongly influenced by their faith. Secondly, it provides a constant challenge to purely secular ethics by insisting that the will of God (however hard it is to discern at times) must be the final arbiter in ethics. In terms of the paradox with which we began this section on religion, Islam would always assert that God's will and command is what *must* be done, and that although human reason may be an aid, it is not in itself enough to guide ethics.

CONCLUSION

In this chapter I have tried to enrich our understanding of bioethics by describing a range of perspectives that are different in approach from a philosophical use of moral theory to deal with moral problems. Inevitably this has meant a very diverse range of material, not all of which may seem relevant for the specific issues that we shall now go on to discuss in the subsequent chapters. However, it is important to recognize that ethical issues are not easily solved simply by a 'knock down' ethical theory or even by some core principles. A major step towards understanding the depth of dilemma in bioethics, but also in understanding how much disagreement there is bound to be in trying to solve these dilemmas, is to see the complexity of the ways in which we all reach individual moral decisions. We need to see where others are coming from in their moral judgements (and also to recognize our own moral blind spots) if we are to have a reasonable and reasoned discussion of the issues. So, recognizing what a range of perspectives there is in actual, rather than purely theoretical, discussions of bioethics might be the first step in reaching some kind of consensus across the social, cultural and religious differences in our globalized world. That, at least, may make the bioethics endeavour worthwhile.

FURTHER READING

You will find a very good range of readings on Feminist Bioethics in Scully, Baldwin-Ragavan and Fitzpatrick (eds), *Feminist Bioethics: At the Centre, on the Margins* (2010). For Care ethics see Campbell (1998). To understand the approaches of Eastern religions to ethics, consult 'The *Dharma* of ethics and ethics of *Dharma*' by Arti Dhand in the *Journal of Religious Ethics* (2002). There are numerous accounts of ethics in the 'Abrahamic' traditions. For a short survey of Christian approaches see Robin Gill, *Health Care and Christian*

Ethics (2006); for a very recent account of Jewish approaches see Alan Mittleman, *A Short History of Jewish Ethics* (2012). Islamic approaches are perhaps best researched using journal articles and Internet resources (see below).

There is a large literature on all the perspectives summarized in this chapter, and so for special topics it may be best to go to websites, especially the very comprehensive one managed by the Joseph and Rose Kennedy Institute of Ethics at Georgetown University (http://bioethics.georgetown.edu/publications/scope-notes/sn38.htm). For the debate about Eastern and Western bioethics and for articles on Islamic, Buddhist and other approaches to bioethics consult the journal *Asian Bioethics Review* (http://www.asianbioethicsreview.com/).

CLINICAL ETHICS

INTRODUCTION

We saw in Chapter 1 how bioethics started with a radical critique of the way in which doctors and other health care professionals were acting ethically (or, at times, unethically). The subject then broadened out to include a wide range of issues related to human health and welfare. In this chapter I shall keep the focus on the practice of medicine and health care and look at the range of difficult moral issues that have been thrown up in clinical practice by the huge advances in medical science and technology. I shall start before birth (with issues to do with the embryo and with new birth technology) and carry on past death (with the debate about the use of human organs and other tissues from the deceased). But first we need to look at the professional relationship between doctors or other health care providers and the patients they serve. What makes this relationship ethical? What are the moral hazards in the health care relationship?

THE CLINICAL RELATIONSHIP – A CONSPIRACY AGAINST THE LAITY?

In his play *The Doctor's Dilemma*, George Bernard Shaw describes the medical relationship as a 'conspiracy against the laity', by which he means that doctors (and other professionals) are in danger of using their special knowledge and power as a way of gaining personal advantage, rather than as a means to help their patients. (Shaw borrowed the phrase from the Scottish philosopher and economist Adam Smith, who used it in his famous book, *The Wealth of Nations*, published in 1776, to describe how professions band together to gain economic advantage.) So how can health professionals demonstrate that this is an unfair description of how they act?

All the medical ethical codes, going back to the ancient Hippocratic Oath and Charaka Samhita's Oath of Initiation (see Appendix), stress that the first consideration of the health professional must always be the best interests and welfare of the patient – but why is it necessary even to stress this, isn't it obvious? The answer lies in the helplessness and fear that people experience when they encounter a major, maybe fatal, illness, or when they are disabled by a serious accident or infection. If you are the victim of a road crash or of an assault, or are rushed into hospital with a heart attack, or if you are told that you have cancer, or AIDS, or some other life-threatening illness, you will probably feel devastated and highly vulnerable, needing to be treated by people whom you can trust totally. This is why clinical ethics matters so much. Of course, we want to be able to trust other professionals also – lawyers, teachers, priests and other professions that deal with our personal affairs. But trust matters most when we are really anxious and unsure about how we can be helped, and it is at such crisis points in our lives that health professionals come in. There are several aspects of the clinical relationship in which this trust can be either justified or betrayed. These are: commitment to our best interests; treating us with dignity and respect; and safeguarding our confidentiality.

BEST INTERESTS

The Geneva Code of Medical Ethics, drawn up in 1948 after the revelation of the medical atrocities of the Second World War, states: 'The health of my patient will be my first consideration.' This echoes the Hippocratic promise that 'The regimen I shall adopt shall be for the benefit of the patients, according to my ability or judgment and not for their hurt or any wrong', and the Samhita's Oath: 'Day and night, however thou mayest be engaged, thou shalt endeavour for the relief of patients with all thy heart and soul. Thou shalt not desert or injure thy patient for the sake of thy life or thy living.' This means that personal profit, or reputation, or the pursuit of research, or serving the needs of government or any other agency, can never be the factor that finally determines a professional decision. The deciding factor must always be the best interests of the patient.

However, deciding what is in the best interests of patients is not always straightforward. Let us imagine several clinical situations in which it could be a problem. In the first situation, an ambulance has been called to a house by a neighbour, who has discovered that a young person in her mid twenties has taken an overdose in an attempt to kill herself. The young woman refuses to go to hospital, saying that all she wants to do is die. What should the paramedics in this situation do? Should they force her to go to hospital, because it is in her best interests? Or should they let her die, as she says she wishes? In the second situation, an elderly, mentally alert patient is advised by her doctors that she must have an amputation of her gangrenous limb, in order to save her life. But she refuses, saying that she would rather die earlier than live the rest of her life with only one leg. Can the doctors overrule her decision and go ahead with the amputation? In the third situation, a university professor has developed advanced dementia. Before this happened, he had said that he would rather die than keep on living without his mental capacities. Now, however, in his demented state, he appears quite happy and unaware of his condition. He develops a lung infection, which could be treated with antibiotics, but should the doctors treat him, knowing his earlier wish?

In all these cases, the same questions arise: who is the best judge of a patient's best interests, and on what basis should the judgement be made? This becomes an acute problem when there is a life-and-death situation and the doctor or health care team believe that the patient's refusal is wrong, that is, not in their best interests. In some situations, this problem can be helped by legislation which allows people to make an advanced declaration, prior to their losing mental capacity, or to appoint a person who is authorized to make such decisions on their behalf. This might help in the third case, in which the choice of death rather than dementia could be respected by not intervening in the illness, except to ensure that the patient was comfortable. (I return to this kind of non-treatment decision later in the chapter, when I discuss end-of-life decisions.) But, what about the suicidal person, or the patient who wants to keep her leg, despite the fatal consequences? Can we say that they are acting against their better judgement, that they don't fully realize what is in their best interests?

Obviously, we need to think very carefully about what we mean by 'best interests'. Is the person himself or herself always the best judge of this? We can all act foolishly or impulsively at times, and then, later, looking back, see that what we did was not in fact the best thing. So, satisfying our wish of the moment may not be the same as looking after our best interests, and this becomes very serious if our refusal of treatment will mean that there is no chance of regretting our decision, since we will be dead! Considerations such as these make it fairly standard practice for health care professionals to intervene to save a life even if – at least at first – the patient is refusing the intervention.

Yet, how can we be *so* sure that the health professional knows better than the patient what is best for him or her? If we think back to the moral theories in Chapter 2, we can see that very different kinds of answer could be given to this question. If it is simply a matter of calculating consequences, then medical expertise can help to a limited extent, since it can show the person just what will happen if they refuse the treatment (for example, refusal of an amputation will probably lead to the infection spreading until it kills the patient). But the health professional cannot say whether – for that *particular* person – the consequences *overall* will be better or worse. Surely, that is for the person to judge. The idea that the doctor always knows best, beyond what is known about the medical facts and consequences, is what is known as *medical paternalism*. The doctor acts as a kind of parent, preventing the patient from acting foolishly, as a father might control a child. But patients are not the children of their doctors, and this means they have a right to take their own decisions, however foolish others may consider them to be. So, this leads us to the notion of autonomy. In this account of best interests, the health professionals can try to advise the patient, can even argue with the patient to be sure that their decision is a fully considered one, but finally the choice is the patient's.

A third way of deciding about best interests comes from the VE approach. In this theory flourishing and fulfilment are the key concepts, so the best interests of the patient will be served by helping them to think through all aspects of their choice in order to see if it accords with those things they most care about or aim for in their lives. For example, if we think of the professor's pre-dementia decision, we can imagine that it was based both on what he most cared about for himself (his intellectual pursuits) and his thoughts of how his state, though no longer known by him, would distress those whom he loved. For the young woman attempting suicide, on the other hand, the wish to die may be related to other, seemingly intractable problems in her life, for which there may be another way out if she is given the time and the help to consider what most matters to her. 'Best interests', then, will always be a complex idea, and one that must be related to the individual patient, not to some preconceived ideas of health professionals about what is best for people.

DIGNITY AND RESPECT

This account of best interests leads on naturally to the quality of the relationship which health care professionals should have with patients. The essence of this is summed up in the phrase 'the patient as a person'. In other words, people should not be treated as though they were merely examples of a disease, as just 'interesting cases'. Respect for the patient as a person means being sensitive to that individual's needs and wishes, and, despite the heavy demands on a health professional's time and attention, taking enough time to listen and to respond appropriately to their concerns and questions. This aspect is especially important when seeking consent for treatment. Taking consent is sometimes seen as simply getting a signature on a consent form, but in fact it should be a process which enables the patient (if competent) to take an active part in the decision. Valid consent has three key features: it is *informed*, *competent* and *voluntary*. We shall consider each of these in turn.

INFORMED CONSENT

How much does a patient need to know in order to make an informed decision about treatment? This is a much-debated question in both medical ethics and medical law. Medicine is a highly technical area, requiring many years of training to become a specialist in a particular field. Thus, there will always be an 'information gap' between the health professional and the patient (though with the advent of the Internet this gap may be closing a little). The responsibility on the health professional is to communicate the essential information to the patient in a language which that person can understand, and to check to see if the patient has understood it. This essential information includes the reason for the proposed treatment, the nature of the treatment, the other treatment options available (if any), the likely effect of the treatment (including adverse effects and risks) and the consequences for the patient if the treatment is not carried out. The most difficult area is deciding which risks, from a possibly very long list, have to be included in the information. This needs to be decided in terms of both the *severity* of the adverse outcome (for example, death or a major disability) and its *probability*. A rule of thumb (backed up by some Court decisions) is that all risks which a 'reasonable person' would wish to know about should be described, but, in addition, that risks which are very significant for that particular person – even if remote – should be mentioned. (For example, a professional athlete would wish to know if there is any risk of loss of agility or balance.)

COMPETENT CONSENT

But what if the patient is not capable of consenting? Competency to consent relates to the capacity of the patient to receive and understand the information, as well as the capacity to retain it and make it the basis for an informed decision. Some patients are clearly incompetent, for example, infants, very young children, unconscious patients and patients with a serious lack of mental capacity through severe intellectual disability, traumatic brain injury or advanced dementia. However, lack of capacity should never be assumed simply on the basis of a medical diagnosis (for example, of mental illness), and careful assessment needs to be made of the competence of the person to make that *specific* decision. In the case of children, although they may be below the age of legal consent (which varies from country to country), they should be involved in major decisions if they are old enough to understand what is involved, and their *assent* should be sought. A patient should not be judged incompetent just because they make what the doctor considers to be a foolish decision. So, in the case of the lady refusing to have an amputation, her refusal is not sufficient reason to judge her to be incompetent, and the operation cannot go ahead without her consent unless other evidence shows that she is incapable of making an informed decision.

VOLUNTARY CONSENT

Thirdly, the decision to consent to treatment must be a genuinely free choice by the patient, not one that they are coerced into making. (If the patient is not given the opportunity to make a free choice and to refuse the intervention, then the health professional could be guilty of the tort (civil offence) of battery.) Unfortunately there are many historical examples of the failure to obtain voluntary consent, not only in research, as described in Chapter 1, but also in treatment. In the early decades of the twentieth century it was common practice in some American states, as well as in several European countries, for the 'feeble minded' and people with a range of mental illnesses to be sterilized without any possibility of their refusing this drastic intervention in their lives (see Black, 2003). But coercion can also be more subtle than this kind of physical compulsion. Sometimes health professionals try to bully patients into complying with their treatment advice, perhaps by implying a withdrawal of other care if they do not comply. Families can also put emotional pressure onto patients to accept treatments when the patient may feel they have had enough. (Examples would be persuading the patient to continue with medication or to undergo radical surgery for cancer, when the patient feels the time has come to die peacefully and without the adverse side-effects of treatment.) In some cultures, however, as we saw in Chapter 3, the wishes of the family will be very important to the patient, and they will want to do what the family as a whole decides. The main requirement is that the patient is left genuinely free to choose, according to their own values. These values can include doing what matters to the family or to other persons close to the patient.

Finally, there will be many situations in the clinical relationship with patients in which the patient never had, or has lost, the capacity to decide. At this point the concept of dignity, described earlier, becomes the central one. Dignity refers to respecting the status of every patient as a fellow human being, however damaged, disabled or incompetent. Modern medical practice can very easily strip the patient of all human dignity. In acute settings, the patient can be reduced to a nearly naked, helpless organism connected to an array of high-tech machines. Of course, such indignity is sometimes necessary in order to save life, but in the case of inevitably dying patients the technology can be allowed to take over, providing futile interventions instead of the sensitive care needed. In the case of long-term care of severely mentally or physically compromised patients, the indignity can occur not from high-tech interventions but from their treatment as 'vegetables', needing to be fed, watered and cleaned, but no longer seen as fellow humans with unique histories and deep feelings. In some care home settings, this attitude is reinforced by physical or **pharmacological constraints**, often used for the convenience of staff rather than to ensure patient safety. The overall result of such approaches to those patients who cannot care for themselves and cannot make decisions about their own treatment is that health professionals become reduced to being mere custodians of bodies which no longer have any value in themselves. This is a serious dereliction of the professional ideal that *every* patient should be treated as a person in their own right.

CONFIDENTIALITY

The final feature of the professional relationship is confidentiality. Health care professionals have privileged access to some of the most private aspects of people's lives. If it is necessary for diagnosis or treatment, they are permitted to see and handle any parts of the patient's body, and they can seek information from the patient about intimate details of their lives. For this reason, confidentiality is one of the cornerstones of health care ethics, and the insistence on maintaining secrecy about the patient begins with the Oath of

Hippocrates and Chakara Samthi Oath. Different reasons can be given for stressing the importance of confidentiality. Perhaps the strongest is that the health professional has a duty to respect the patient's privacy and autonomy, because of the trust patients place in their helpers when they pass on personal information. The health professional breaches that trust if the information is passed on to others who do not need it in order to care effectively for the patient. (Trust is not breached if the patient has specifically consented to this disclosure, for example, for health research purposes.) There is also a consequentialist argument for maintaining confidentiality. If patients know that their information is not protected but might be passed on to others, then they might conceal some important facts from health professionals, or they might lose trust in them such that they would no longer consult them at all, leading to serious risks to their health and, in some cases, to the health of others. (A good example of this would be concealing information about sexually transmitted infections.)

Of course, confidentiality does not mean that *only* the person to whom the information is given is allowed to know the details. Health care professionals work in teams and the relevant information about patients needs to be known by the whole team, and also by any health professional to whom the patient is referred. Without this internal flow of information patients could receive inappropriate or even dangerous treatment. However, information should be divulged on a 'need to know' basis, and some personal details revealed to a practitioner may be intended only for him or her and not be relevant to the patient's on-going care. For this reason, practitioners need to think carefully about what should be entered into the medical record, since this is what will be more generally available to other practitioners. (On the other hand, a patient cannot require that something is excluded from the record, if that information is clearly necessary to ensure effective treatment in the future.)

Although confidentiality is very important, there are times when it may have to be breached, either because there are laws which require the information to be passed on (for example, laws governing the reporting of some infectious diseases which could spread to other people) or because there is a real risk of harm to others if the information is kept secret. A famous illustration of the second reason for disclosing information is the Tarasoff case, which was heard in various California Courts (and finally in that state's Supreme Court) in the 1970s. Tatiana Tarasoff was murdered by her former boyfriend after she had broken up with him. The boyfriend had told his counsellor of his intention to kill her, and the counsellor had warned the campus police that he might be a risk and should be confined in a psychiatric hospital. However, the police took no action other than interviewing the boyfriend and, unaware of the specific threat, they did not detain him. The Supreme Court held that counsellors or psychiatrists had a duty to warn either the intended victim or the police of such specific threats and to ensure that the intended victim was protected. This ruling leads to a general principle, which is that confidentiality should be breached when there is a clear threat to a specific individual. Another example of this is when an HIV positive person refuses to inform a sexual partner of the diagnosis. Ideally, the person should be persuaded to tell their partner. If this is not done, then the health practitioner has to inform the partner, but only after telling the infected person of the intended action. Other examples involve informing the relevant authorities, for example, when the medical condition of a driver could lead to dangerous driving, or when information relevant to a serious crime (such as murder or rape) needs to be passed on to the police. These, however, are all unusual and exceptional circumstances. In nearly all situations, the 'sacred trust' between practitioner and patient should never be betrayed, and secrets should be kept.

LIFE BEFORE BIRTH

Having described the essential characteristics of the relationship between health professionals and their patients, we now go on to look at specific topics in medical ethics, beginning with dilemmas in reproductive medicine. This is one of the most controversial areas in clinical ethics, in which there is often radical (and perhaps irreconcilable) disagreement.

TERMINATION OF PREGNANCY (ABORTION)

The question of whether it is morally permissible to terminate the life of a foetus, and, if so, at what stage of development and for what reasons, has led in some countries to a polarization of views into two camps, the 'right to life' versus 'the woman's right to choose'. The controversy has been so extreme in some places that clinics have been violently attacked and practitioners practising abortion have been murdered. Religion has played a prominent part in this debate (though not all religious believers totally oppose abortion). The teaching of the Roman Catholic Church that the embryo is a person 'from the moment of conception' has led some groups to describe abortion as 'murder of the innocent'. Some other religious groups – evangelical Christians, Orthodox Jews and some Muslim scholars – also condemn abortion outright or restrict it to a very few situations, such as clear risk to the life of the mother or pregnancy after rape. Yet, as we saw in Chapter 3, there is no single ethical view in this or in other areas which represents the beliefs of all followers of a particular religious faith. Even in the case of the Roman Catholic Church, the teaching that the embryo/foetus is a person from the moment of conception dates as far back as only the nineteenth century, when Pope Pius IX made an *ex cathedra* statement to this effect. According to Catholic teaching such statements are infallible, and so no subsequent pope has departed from this claim. However, earlier the Catholic Church held a similar position to that of Jewish tradition, that ensoulment occurs much later, at the time of 'quickening', when the mother feels the baby moving in her womb.

Many ethical issues, including the question of the morality of abortion, revolve round disagreement about the status of the embryo/foetus. The problem is that this is never simply a matter of scientific description. The term 'person' is an evaluative, not a descriptive term. It represents a *claim* about the *status* of the cluster of cells at the beginning of human life. Some opponents of abortion argue that, because the entity created at conception is genetically unique (resulting from a combination of the genes of the two parents), it must be seen as an individual person. However, this causes numerous conceptual difficulties because of the major loss of fertilized eggs at menstruation if they do not implant in the uterus (yet no one mourns for each of these), the splitting of some embryos to create identical twins (so not one individual after all?) and the failure of some implanted embryos to develop human characteristics, instead becoming a non-malignant tumour (a teratoma). Thus, for some supporters of abortion, the embryo/ foetus is better seen as the (likely) beginnings of one or more human lives – as *nascent human life*, but still far short of individual human existence as a person. This approach (sometimes called the gradualist view) regards the foetus as having increasing moral significance as it develops more and more human characteristics. So, we should always have 'respect for foetal life' in the light of its potential to become a person, but we need not afford it the full protection we give to a newly born child. This gradualist account entails identifying certain key points in foetal development to decide what is morally permitted. For example, the 14th day after conception, when the beginnings of human life are seen in the 'primitive streak' (the precursor of the spinal cord), can be used as a cut-off point for using the embryo in research and extracting stem cells from it (see a discussion of this later in the chapter); and 'viability', the point in gestation when survival outside the womb is technically possible (occurring round about the 23rd to 25th week), can be used as a restriction on the range of justifiable reasons for abortion.

This gradualist approach can be criticized from both the 'right' and the 'left'. Those who want an absolute ban on abortion point out that gestation is a smooth development, with no real transition points, so trying to fix personal value later than conception will always be arbitrary. Better, they say, to take the clear beginning at conception as the only secure criterion for the full humanity of the embryo. On the other hand, some advocates for abortion on demand take the developmental argument further, claiming that 'personhood' (seen in terms of self-awareness and the capacity for valuing one's own life) does not begin even at birth, but requires months or even years of postnatal development. Thus, these critics of gradualism see no need to draw a line between abortion and infanticide, advocating both as potential choices of the parents.

As noted earlier, the different moral positions in this debate appear to be irreconcilable. It becomes important, however, not to allow the debate to focus solely on the foetus, thereby forgetting that we are discussing a maternal–foetal co-existence, ending only at birth (or earlier through spontaneous or induced abortion). How do we describe correctly the moral dilemmas of the women in this situation? (Women readers might remark at this point that men, including the author of this book, often overlook this aspect, or suppose that they can speak authoritatively about women's choices – like the (male) pope!) There are many reasons that can lead a pregnant woman to consider having an abortion. At one extreme, there is pregnancy following rape and pregnancy of an underage girl as a result of sexual abuse by a male relative. Then, there are situations where continuation of the pregnancy is a serious threat to the woman's physical health (for example, because of a heart condition) or to her mental health. The potential disability of the future child is another factor which can influence the decision, and prenatal tests and ultrasound scans are now available to predict this. There can also be what are sometimes called 'social reasons', for example, the woman may be unsupported and unable to care for a child on her own, or the family may be too poor to support another child, or the foetus may be of the 'wrong' gender, or the pregnancy was unintended and will interfere with the woman's future plans.

Clearly, some of these reasons seem more morally compelling than others. For example, many people would feel that social inconvenience is a weak justification for ending a potential human life. On the other hand, those who advocate an absolute prohibition on abortion are committed to insisting that even a child impregnated by her own father must endure nine months of pregnancy followed by childbirth before (presumably) having to give up the baby for adoption or residential care. The absolutist prohibition also encourages some women to risk death for an unborn child, even though there may be other children dependent on her. Many writers see such a view as a gross infringement on the rights of women and girls to make choices about their own bodies and about their present and future health, and so advocate no restrictions on abortion at least in the first trimester (three months) of pregnancy, when the foetus is well short of viability. There are also strong consequentialist arguments against a total ban on abortions, since in countries where this is the legal situation there is a high incidence of 'back street' abortions, leading to the serious illness and death of a large number of women.

On the other hand, does the total dependence of the foetus on the woman for survival put a special moral obligation on her to protect this life? The philosopher Judith Jarvis Thomson (Thomson, 1971) has used an analogy to argue that this is not so. Imagine, she says, that you wake up one day to discover that while you were asleep your body has been hooked up to that of a world-famous violinist. His kidneys have failed, but if he remains connected to you for nine months, he will fully recover and you can be disconnected! Would you have an absolute moral obligation to agree to remaining connected? Thomson argues that, though it would be a praiseworthy thing to do, you surely do have the right to refuse to have your body used in this way. So, she concludes, even if those who say the embryo is fully a person from conception are correct, it does not follow that the pregnant woman would be morally wrong to end the pregnancy. She would still have the right to choose.

Philosophers often make up strange stories to prove a point! But the violinist analogy does make us think how it could possibly be justifiable to enforce the continuation of a pregnancy and the pain of childbirth on women for whom this is unacceptable, and who may not in any case have chosen to become pregnant. On the other hand, as the pregnancy progresses and the foetus becomes more and more like a tiny baby, with reactions to stimuli and at least some form of pain perception, a decision to end its life must always be a hard moral choice. So, the gradualist position, despite its ambiguities, may be the best source for formulating laws and for guiding women and their medical advisors in the choices to be made.

ASSISTED REPRODUCTION

At the opposite end of the spectrum from those who may decide to end a pregnancy are those who are desperate to achieve it! Infertility in both men and women is a source of great distress to many people and they will go to great lengths to overcome it. Over the past few decades, assisted reproductive technology (ART) has thrown up an amazing range of new possibilities for achieving this. At the simplest level, artificial insemination (AI), using sperm either from the woman's partner or from a donor, can achieve fertilization of the woman's ova within her own body, and may be self-administered (the so called 'turkey baster' method). But many more possibilities are opened up with the development of *in vitro* (in glass) fertilization (IVF), in which sperm and egg are brought together in a laboratory environment after being harvested from the male and female bodies. IVF produces what the media have called 'test tube babies', but, in fact, the babies do not develop in a test tube or in any other external place, but within a woman's body, after one or more fertilized eggs have been re-implanted.

ONE BABY – FIVE PARENTS?

These new techniques have brought help to huge numbers of childless couples worldwide, but they also open up a whole range of possibilities that bring new social and ethical dilemmas. Unlike traditional ways of producing offspring through sexual intercourse between a man and a woman, it is now perfectively possible to make a complete separation between the couple or individual seeking a child, the source of the sperm and eggs from which the child is created and the birth mother of the child. Sperm, eggs and embryos can be frozen for later use, and the woman in whose body the embryo is implanted need not have any genetic relationship to it. Thus, a baby could have five parents: the couple who 'commission' the child, but do not provide either the eggs or the sperm (known collectively as gametes), the man and the woman who donate the gametes (and who may remain anonymous) and the surrogate mother, in whom the embryo is placed and who subsequently gives birth to the baby. Moreover, these techniques allow other possibilities, such as a single woman becoming pregnant without having sexual intercourse with the genetic father, a postmenopausal woman becoming pregnant, using a donated embryo (and possibly being the surrogate mother for her own daughter), a female homosexual couple arranging the pregnancy of one partner, using donated sperm, and a male homosexual couple using a surrogate mother to produce a child genetically related to one of them.

Such complications have led some countries to create specific laws (sometimes also with oversight bodies) to regulate these new birth technologies, but in other countries there is no legislation or regulation, and so all the listed possibilities become solely a matter of 'consumer' choice, with – in some places, such as in some American states – no ban on trading in gametes or paying for surrogacy services. Thus, advertisements appear for 'desirable' products – for example, sperm from Nobel laureates, or eggs from intelligent and beautiful young women. There are a number of ethical concerns raised by these developments. These are: effect on family life; welfare of the child; and the prospect of 'designer babies'.

The Roman Catholic Church has been at the forefront of opposition to nearly all of these technological developments, partly on the grounds that they may entail destruction of some embryos, but also because they are a departure from 'natural procreation' and, so, a threat to family life and to the welfare of children. We recall from the previous chapter that the Catholic tradition, based on the teaching of Thomas Aquinas, promotes the idea of Natural Law. This describes certain inherent requirements built into the natural world, including our human nature, that guide and restrict our actions according to what God intended us to be and do. Knowing the Natural Law, so the teaching goes, does not require religious faith: it can be discerned by any rational person. When this is applied to sexual intercourse and procreation, the Catholic Church teaches that it is wrong to interfere with the requirement that children are the product of a monogamous union between a man and a woman. So the church forbids the use of methods that can result in the variety of ways of producing offspring described earlier. The only form of ART that might be permissible is insemination using the husband's sperm, but even this should be avoided if at all possible. Moreover, only 'natural' means of contraception are allowed, and this means that all contraceptive methods are prohibited, except the 'rhythm method', which tries to prevent conception by avoiding intercourse when the woman is ovulating. (The combination of this opposition to most contraception and the condemnation of abortion results in a very high rate of dangerous and sometimes fatal back-street abortions in many Catholic countries (BBC, 2009a, CBS News Staff, 2012, *The Economist*, 2007).)

To non-Catholics these teachings may seem strange, since it can be pointed out that all human activity is a combination of the 'natural' and the technologically altered. Is it only 'natural' for us to walk or run, for example – leading to a disapproval of all forms of vehicular transport? It is clear that 'natural' is rather like the word 'person', as discussed earlier: it is an evaluative term, not a simple description, since it picks out certain human capacities as the way things *ought* to be and brands others as against nature. On the other hand, ART has clearly disrupted what used to be (in some cultures at least) the standard family unit of mother, father and children, and this could be seen as a risk to the emotional well-being of children. Should there be concern for the welfare of children brought up with two parents of the same sex, or with one parent only, or with both a social or commissioning mother and a birth mother?

However, it seems that this may not really be a justifiable concern, since there is a lack of evidence to show that children are best born and brought up in the traditional heterosexual, two-parent unit. Quite apart from assisted reproduction, there are many examples of children growing up in one-parent or same-sex parents households, or of having a birth mother who is different from their social mother. These come about from bereavement, divorce, custody being given to a parent in a homosexual household and adoption (which, in some countries, can include adoption by single persons or by gay couples). Sometimes, too, traditional family structures fail to be supportive of the children (who are seen merely as a nuisance by the adults), and they can, in some cases, conceal severe physical and sexual abuse. It may be, then, that the key factor ensuring welfare is not the *form* of the relationship, but the emotional environment of the child's upbringing. A child conceived by artificial means is very likely to be ardently wanted, and so brought up in a caring and loving atmosphere.

But now another ethical problem may arise: will the child be seen as valuable in its own right, or no more than a way of satisfying the needs of its parents? (Such a question may arise particularly strongly when conceptions in elderly people mean that early in its life the child will probably lose at least one parent.) Are children to be seen as simply desirable products, made available by the new market in assisted reproduction?

DESIGNER BABIES

This question becomes more acute when we consider one more outcome from the development of IVF – the possibility of selecting which embryo(s) to implant, following genetic tests of their potential, a technique called Pre-implantation Genetic Diagnosis (PGD). This technique was developed as a way of preventing the birth of babies likely to inherit a disease from their parents (cystic fibrosis is one example). Using PGD, the affected embryos, and also embryos which are carriers of the disease, can be identified and only non-affected embryos considered for implantation. But the technique could be used for many other purposes, of which the most obvious would be selecting an embryo of the desired sex. This function could be extended, especially if donated gametes were used, to aim for children with specific height, eye colour, intelligence and other characteristics. If one added to this genetic selection genetic manipulation of the embryos to remove some features and enhance others, we arrive at 'designer babies' – 'the baby you have dreamed of having!'

Some theorists fail to see any problem in such a development. Those in the libertarian camp stress the notion of 'reproductive autonomy', arguing that, provided there is no evidence of actual harm to the future child, the commissioning of a particular kind of child is a private matter and should be left to parents, without any interference by the state. The ethical concern, however, can be expressed in the term 'commodification'. The child, instead of being valued in its own right, is turned into a possession of the parents and required to fit their expectations of the ideal child. (Such a hope does seem doomed to failure, given that genetics is just one aspect of how a person develops!) For both deontological and VE theory, parenthood is not seen as type of ownership but, rather, as a role or vocation, carrying both duties and unexpected opportunities for happiness and fulfilment for both child and parents (Murray, 1996). This is all summed up in the words of the poet Kahlil Gibran:

> Your children are not your children.
> They are the sons and daughters of Life's longing for itself.
> They come through you but not from you,
> And though they are with you, yet they belong not to you.
> You may give them your love but not your thoughts.
> For they have their own thoughts.
> You may house their bodies but not their souls,

For their souls dwell in the house of tomorrow, which you cannot visit,
    not even in your dreams.
You may strive to be like them, but seek not to make them like you.
For life goes not backward nor tarries with yesterday.
You are the bows from which your children as living arrows are sent
    forth.

(Gibran, 1980, first published 1923)

TRANSPLANTATION AND REGENERATIVE MEDICINE

ORGAN TRANSPLANTATION

In 1967 the South African surgeon Christian Barnard performed the
first successful human-to-human heart transplantation. Although
the recipient lived for only two weeks, there was international
excitement at the new possibilities for survival opened up by organ
transplantation. (Successful kidney transplantations had in fact
been carried out a decade earlier, but it was the drama of replacing
a faulty human heart that caught worldwide attention.) Since
those early days, the possibilities for transplantation have expanded
dramatically, covering a range of organs – kidneys, liver, pancreas,
heart and lung, intestine and thymus. (In addition, the range of
tissue transplantation has greatly increased, in including corneas
and – most controversially – faces.) Survival rates have also steadily
improved with the refinement of methods of preventing rejection
of the transplant, and in some cases a second operation has been
performed when the first transplant eventually fails.

However, the success of organ transplantation has brought with
it major ethical problems. As demand for organs has escalated,
partly caused by the increase in chronic diseases such as diabetes,
the supply of organs is falling dramatically short of meeting the
need. For example, in the USA it has been estimated that about
10 people die every day while waiting for a transplant, while the
figures in China are even more dramatic, with 1.5 million patients
needing a transplant, but only 10,000 operations performed
annually. In the cases of the kidney and the liver, live donors can be
used, since a person can survive with one kidney and, if a portion
of the liver is donated, it will subsequently grow back. (Later in the
chapter I shall be discussing problems in obtaining organs from

the deceased.). The success rate for live donation is higher than for donation from the deceased, but it also raises major problems to do with exploitation and consent. Some donors are relatives or friends of the recipient, and although this may entail fewer problems, there will always be the question of undue emotional pressure on the donor, especially in some cultures where filial duty is seen as a major value. (Thus, living donors may come disproportionately from among female family members (Biller-Andorno, 2002).) The concerns are even greater if living *unrelated* donors are used, since these nearly all come from impoverished countries, in which the 'donors' may be struggling to survive or to pay back huge burdens of debt. There is plenty of evidence of a worldwide trade in organs, with 'health brokers' obtaining organs from the poor to meet the needs of the rich. Large sums of money change hands, but very little of this goes to the 'donor', and in most cases the poverty is only temporarily relieved, if at all, and the donor's health and prospects for employment are often severely affected.

Some writers have suggested that the problems of organ shortage and of the exploitation of the poor can be met by the introduction of a 'regulated market', in which a fair price is paid, the donor's health is safeguarded and the organs obtained are given to those most in need. However, it is impossible to see how such a market could be implemented and properly regulated, given that organ trading is not restricted to one country or region, but is a highly profitable worldwide enterprise, crossing many national boundaries and responding to an ever-increasing demand. Thus international organizations, such as the WHO and the WMA have been uncompromising in their opposition to any form of organ trading, allowing only reimbursement of documented expenses. The guiding principle was spelled out in the Declaration of Istanbul as follows:

> Organ trafficking and transplant tourism violate the principles of equity, justice and respect for human dignity and should be prohibited. Because transplant commercialism targets impoverished and otherwise vulnerable donors, it leads inexorably to inequity and injustice and should be prohibited.
>
> (Participants in the International Summit on Transplant Tourism and Organ Trafficking 2008)

REGENERATIVE MEDICINE

Clearly, the dilemmas of organ donation would be avoided if other ways could be found to replace or repair the damaged body parts. Here, hope has come from advances in culturing and growing the 'building blocks' of all organic tissue – pluripotent stem cells. These have the potential to develop into many different cell types in the body. They also serve as a sort of internal repair system, constantly dividing to replenish other cells as long as the person or animal is still alive. When a stem cell divides, each new cell has the potential either to remain a stem cell or to become another type of cell with a more specialized function, such as a muscle cell, a red blood cell or a brain cell. Stem cells which are pluripotent are capable of differentiating into a wide range of tissues, and so will be of most use in a move towards therapy such as repair of damaged tissues or even the creation of replacement organs. Until recently it was thought that the best source for such primitive and adaptable cells was the human embryo in the very early stage of development, but recently new techniques have been developed that can allow pluripotent cells to be derived from adult (somatic) cells. These are known as iPSCs. Another technique, called **Somatic Cell Nuclear Transfer** (SCNT) – popularly described as 'therapeutic cloning' – can produce pluripotent cells derived from the patient's own somatic cells. The cell nucleus is inserted into an ovum from which the nucleus has been removed and then, using a technique similar to that which produced Dolly the cloned sheep, the process of cell division is stimulated. This technique has obvious therapeutic potential, since it can produce stem cells which are wholly compatible with the patient, thus overcoming the problems of graft rejection that are common in transplantation medicine.

The advance of **regenerative medicine** (sometimes also called 'cell therapy') raises great prospects for effective therapies across an amazing range of medical conditions. However, it also provokes some major ethical issues. The first of these has strongly affected the advance of this area in the USA, since it has become a major political debating point. The extraction of stem cells from a three- to five-day-old embryo, or the creation of a cloned embryo through SCNT, inevitably entails the use of embryos solely as a means to advance research or therapy, and also entails the destruction of the embryo once the cells have been extracted. As we saw in the previous section, some groups regard the embryo as having the full status of a person, and so these techniques are regarded as immoral, breaking the dictum of Immanuel Kant that we should never use persons as 'mere means'. It may be that this controversy will be short-lived, if the technique of inducing adult cells to become pluripotent proves fully effective. For the present, however, most scientists believe that work with embryonic cells needs to continue if we are to fully understand the processes and develop fully effective therapies. Thus, this conflict, like the conflict over abortion, is likely to continue for some years to come.

But there is another major ethical issue currently affecting regenerative medicine. This issue can be described as 'turning hope into hype'. Throughout the world, extravagant claims are being made for stem cell therapy, and large sums are being extracted from desperate patients, when there is virtually no evidence that safe and effective methods have been established to achieve any sort of cure or even amelioration of their condition. Part of the difficulty has been that governments have been slow to regulate this new field and have not applied the same stringent conditions of prior research and post-marketing surveillance that apply to pharmaceuticals and medical devices. Regenerative medicine does seem to hold out great hope for the future, but, for the present, the shortcomings and ethical uncertainties associated with transplantation and other proven therapies seem likely to remain.

MENTAL HEALTH

Most health care practitioners, whatever their speciality, will encounter issues related to mental health in the course of their career. It is estimated that neuropsychiatric disorders contribute to 13 per cent of the global burden of disease (WHO Department of Mental Health and Substance Abuse, 2011). One of the most common forms of mental illness is depression, but there is a wide range of other disorders, including **schizophrenia, cyclothymic mood disorder** (sometimes called manic depressive psychosis), eating disorders (anorexia and **bulimia**) and neurotic disorders, such as **obsessive compulsive disorder, phobias** and panic episodes. In addition, there are the personality disorders, often hardest to diagnose and to treat, of which the best known is the psychopathic personality, a person prone to violence and antisocial behaviour, with no evidence of normal feelings of remorse. Many mental illnesses are chronic, with symptom management through medication the only treatment option, and some (such as the eating disorders and depression) can be fatal.

MAD, BAD OR SAD?

The ethical issues in dealing with mental illness relate to two different concerns: the welfare of the patient and the safety of others. These problems are made greater by the stigma associated with this type of illness and an exaggerated public perception of the dangerousness of those suffering from some forms of mental disorder. Most countries have legislation designed to deal with these two concerns. The most striking difference from the treatment of physical illness is that the legislation can prevent a person from refusing treatment and can mandate compulsory detention in a mental hospital, if there is evidence of danger to self or others. A basic assumption here is that mental illness can cause a person to be 'out of his mind' ('mad'), and so decisions about what is in the best interests of this patient have to be made by others, since the illness takes away the competence to consent to or refuse treatment. Equally, the patient may be a danger to self, and liable to commit suicide ('sad'), but this self-destructive urge can be alleviated or removed by appropriate treatment. Finally, the patient may commit serious acts of violence ('bad'), possibly under the influence of **paranoid delusions** or through the urging of imagined voices or because of an inability to realize the wrongness of the actions being committed (personality disorder). Mental health legislation, and also criminal procedures legislation, can require compulsory assessment, treatment and detention; and, in the case of very serious crimes, continued detention in a secure psychiatric facility without limit of time. In all these respects, the treatment of mental illness differs strongly both from the treatment of physical illness and from the trial and sentencing of criminals who are found to be of sound mind.

The ethical challenge in this field is getting the balance right between individual freedom and social control. Some states have used a fictitious diagnosis of mental illness to lock up political dissidents indefinitely. Some other societies – at least in the past – have treated the mentally ill as sources of mockery and amusement, detaining them in appalling conditions and making no effort to understand or cure their illness. (The origin of the word 'bedlam' is the English hospital for the insane, the Bethlem Royal Hospital, which dates back to the Middle Ages and was notorious for its cruel and degrading treatment of its unfortunate inmates.) Current approaches to these very widespread illnesses are clearly much more humane, and many effective therapies have been found, especially for depression, the most common of the illnesses. However, the social stigma remains, and a major ethical challenge is finding ways in which the person can be helped back to a state where they feel in control of their lives and can feel once more a sense of self-worth and of social acceptance.

THE END OF LIFE

Despite the illusion sometimes created by modern medicine that even death can be defeated (I shall discuss this idea further in the next chapter), the current reality is that all humans die, sooner or later. So the question is not *whether* we shall die, but *when* and *how* we shall die. Much of this is not under our control either, but nevertheless medical interventions can make a significant difference both to how long we survive and to the quality of life we have in these final days. Clear examples of the differences being made by the rise of scientific medicine are the dramatic increase in life expectancy over the past century, particularly in the more developed regions, where life expectancy was 66 years old in 1950–55, increasing to 77.1 years in 2005–10 (United Nations Population Division, 2009), and the fact that more deaths now occur in hospitals rather than at home – for example 64 per cent to 76 per cent deaths are institutional deaths in England and Wales (Gomes and Higginson, 2008).

However, such changes are not necessarily all positive gains, if we consider not just the length of life that people have, but its quality and also the manner in which they die. That is why there is much debate surrounding the following ethical issues related to the end of life: communicating a bad **prognosis**; humane care of the dying (palliative care); decisions to withhold or withdraw treatment; and decisions deliberately to end a life (euthanasia).

TRUTH TELLING

The traditional medical approach to communicating a bad prognosis (and one which is still common in some cultures, especially in Asia) is for the doctor to inform the relatives of the patient, but to conceal the seriousness of the outlook for survival from the patient him or herself. The reason given for this is that a person, knowing they are likely to die soon, will 'give up hope'. There are several problems with this argument. The first is that concealing the truth from the patient can create a kind of charade, in which the family pretend to be cheerful and hopeful, when in fact they are grieving for the future loss. It is most unlikely that the patient will fail to notice this, especially when the medical approach is also likely to have changed, given the ineffectiveness of treatment. So the person's last days are marred by a secret, preventing open communication between the patient and those caring for the patient. A second problem is that there is no evidence to suggest that when patients are told the truth about their condition they either fare worse or die sooner. On the contrary, the anxiety created by the unacknowledged secret and the uncertainty about just what is going to happen to them is just as likely to have a detrimental effect as is a truthful explanation. A third problem relates to the ethical concept of autonomy. Patients who are deprived of accurate knowledge about their condition have no opportunity to make moral choices about their future (however brief that may be). Instead of being able to put their affairs in order and make their own wishes known about any further medical interventions, they are in danger of being manipulated according to what others judge is best for them. Often, too, the truth is concealed not out of consideration for the patient at all, but to save the family and the health professionals the pain of communicating bad news. (Many doctors, at least in the past, lacked the skills and training needed to communicate sensitively and clearly with people in this situation.)

Of course, these reasons do not justify clumsy and inappropriate communication of bad news, to either patients or relatives, based on the idea that there is some kind of absolute obligation to reveal everything immediately, regardless of the consequences. (We recall Kant's insistence on telling a murderer where his victim is, discussed in Chapter 2.) There are a number of key factors that mean caution is required and time is needed. For some cultures the very mention of death is seen as dangerous and 'tempting fate', and often the subject will need to be approached indirectly and with full involvement of the family. It is also important to sense from the patient how much they wish to be told, and to give information as it is asked for, possibly not revealing a terminal diagnosis if the patient seems to prefer not getting the full medical picture. In addition, predictions in medicine are notoriously difficult, so statements like 'you have six months to live' should be avoided! The key ethical guideline here is that the truth comes through a genuine and trustworthy relationship (Bok, 1978) and that there is never an attempt deliberately to deceive the other person.

PALLIATIVE MEDICINE

When a terminal illness is diagnosed, the focus changes from cure to appropriate care. It has been shown through much research (Missler et al., 2011, Cicirelli, 2001, Hallberg, 2004) that people's fears are not so much about death itself, but about the process of dying. They fear that their last days will be filled with anxiety, pain, breathlessness, loneliness and the indignity of being hooked up to machines that prevent them from communicating with the people they love. The development of the Hospice Movement, started by the British doctor Cecily Saunders, has led to a whole new medical speciality, Palliative Medicine. The Hospice Movement has been committed to achieving 'death with dignity', by developing ways of dealing effectively with the pain, breathlessness and nausea often associated with death from cancer and other terminal illnesses, and by creating appropriate care environments (often called 'hospices'), in which the patient can spend ample time with family, away from the technological and regimented atmosphere of acute hospital wards. Related to this has been the development of home care services, allowing people to spend some or all of their last days in a setting they know and love.

One of the most important findings from research into palliative medicine is that, when the right environment is created and when pain-killing and sedative drugs are administered appropriately, people become less dependent on high doses of medication to achieve a state of comfort and freedom from the fear of unbearable pain. (There are a few exceptions to this, however, which I discuss in the section on euthanasia, later in the chapter.) Thus, palliative medicine helps people to recover what has been called the 'art of dying' (*ars moriendi*), and it has encouraged both patients and health professionals to see terminal illness not as a defeat but as an opportunity to bring a life to a satisfactory ending. Thus, both VE (discussed in Chapter 2) and Care ethics (discussed in Chapter 3) have the most relevance for this field, and for many people the hope and comfort provided by their religious faith can help them to see death as a friend rather than an enemy, when the pain and indignity of dying can be overcome.

TO TREAT OR NOT TO TREAT?

Once we accept that death can be seen as a fulfilment of life, and not merely as a medical defeat, the question of whether to withhold or withdraw treatment, even though that treatment might prolong survival, immediately arises. As we saw earlier, when discussing consent, a competent patient has a right to refuse any treatment, life saving or not, and no one can force that person to accept the treatment, even if the relatives or the health professionals believe that it would be effective. But more difficult ethical and legal issues arise when the patient lacks competence to decide. For example, a baby might be born after 24 weeks of gestation and require treatment in a neonatal intensive care unit in order to survive. However, the prospects are very poor for infants of that gestational age, with a high rate of subsequent death and, among those who do survive, a high rate of mental and physical disability. Parents are usually regarded as the best judges of what is in the best interests of their children – but how are they to decide? At the other end of life, an elderly person who has lost mental capacity may be admitted to hospital with a severe stroke and a number of other serious medical conditions which will make their ability ever to recover and leave hospital extremely unlikely. If they suffer a heart attack, should the staff attempt to resuscitate the patient?

In discussing such difficult cases, reference can be made to the concept of 'medical futility'. If the aim of medical interventions is to maintain or restore health, then what is the point of interventions that will be very unlikely to achieve any successful long-term outcome for the patient? Why prolong the inevitable, instead of ensuring that the person is given appropriate terminal care? So, calling an intervention 'medically futile' is a way of saying that the burden on the patient of starting or continuing treatment is far greater than any possible gain in quality or continuation of life. Cardiac resuscitation provides a good example of this, since it is a very aggressive procedure, often causing injury such as broken ribs, yet with a very poor prospect of success in most patients on whom it is attempted. For this reason, hospitals, after consulting the patient, if competent, and (sometimes) the relatives, may put Do Not Attempt Resuscitation (DNAR) orders in some patients' records. Yet, of course, the decision is never an easy one, since, in a few unusual cases, the patient may get better – a few very premature babies may survive, and live happy lives, and some older people may make an unexpected recovery, leaving hospital to live more years with their family. There is no escape from this uncertainty in medicine. Decisions have to be made on a balance of probabilities – but always insisting on intervention, whatever the odds, can merely result in prolonged and miserable deaths for many patients.

EUTHANASIA

Discussions of non-treatment lead naturally on to the topic of euthanasia. The term literally means just 'dying well' or 'a good death', but most people use it to mean *causing* a death (for good reasons), or 'mercy killing'. Some writers have distinguished between 'passive' and 'active' euthanasia, using the first term to describe what I have just discussed, that is, not treating a person, even though that will, or may, result in their death. 'Active' euthanasia, on the other hand, entails deliberately killing another person, for example, by administering lethal drugs or by injecting air into their veins. This may be at the request of the person (*voluntary active euthanasia*), without the consent of a person who is competent to consent (*involuntary active euthanasia*), or done to a person (for example, a neonate) who is incapable of giving or refusing consent (*non-voluntary active euthanasia*). Another practice, which is part of the same debate, is Physician Assisted Suicide (PAS). In this case, the doctor gives the means of ending life to the patient (usually a lethal dose of drugs), but the patient can choose whether or not to take the lethal dose.

In most, but not all countries, both active euthanasia and PAS are illegal, and euthanasia is seen as equivalent to murder. However, in the American states of Oregon, Montana and Washington, PAS has been made legal for competent adults, and in the European countries the Netherlands, Belgium and Luxembourg, voluntary active euthanasia is also legal, under strict conditions to ensure valid consent. I shall now look at arguments for and against changing the law in this way.

ACTS AND OMISSIONS

Some proponents of euthanasia argue that the law already sanctions euthanasia in the form of withdrawing or withholding life-saving treatment. A famous case is that of Anthony Bland, who was crushed in the Hillsborough football disaster and was for several years in a PVS. The Courts in the UK eventually allowed his doctors to withdraw the artificial hydration and nutrition, which was keeping him alive, on the grounds that this was a medical treatment that was merely prolonging his death. So, if this omission is allowed ('passive euthanasia'), the argument runs, why not the quicker and more humane act of killing him? What is the moral or legal difference between an act and an omission, when both result in death?

Arguments for holding on to the distinction are of two kinds. The first is based in the agent's intention and is known as the Doctrine of Double Effect. This doctrine makes a distinction between *foreseeing* an outcome and *intending* it. So, if decisions not to treat or to discontinue treatment are taken only because to treat would impose a burden on the patient and will bring no lasting benefit, then the action is morally permissible. The death of the patient may be foreseen as a likely outcome, but that is not what is intended by the omission. In a similar way, drugs can be given to relieve a person's pain, even though this may hasten death, but if a massive dose is given (showing that the intention was to end the life, not merely to relieve the pain), then that is equivalent to killing the patient.

A second argument for retaining the acts/omissions distinction is that if we were to be held responsible for *all* the results of our omissions, we would all be constantly guilty of causing deaths! For example, failure to give enough to food aid can result in many deaths in a time of famine in Africa. So did we kill these people? Of course, people are culpable for some omissions, if the actions omitted are part of their responsibility. For example, if I omit to feed my children, when I have the means to do so, and allow them to starve to death, I am clearly culpable. So, in the case of a health care professional, there is a duty to care for patients and to provide adequate treatment, but that does not extend to providing treatment that is considered futile or ineffective.

A RIGHT TO DIE?

A second argument for voluntary euthanasia and PAS is that people have the right to choose the manner and moment of their death, and if they are not capable of bringing this about themselves, either because they do not have effective means or are rendered incapable by their illness, then health professionals (provided they themselves have no conscientious objections) should be allowed to ensure it, without being found guilty of a criminal offence. Some arguments against this viewpoint are based on religious belief. According to several religions, such as Christianity, Islam, Judaism and Sikhism, life and death are in the hands of God, and so individuals have no right to arrange their death or to kill themselves. (This is often referred to as the doctrine of the Sanctity of Life.) But there is also an argument against legalizing euthanasia, on grounds of human rights. Whose rights should we be considering when we plan to make it easier for people to be killed at their own request? Arguments against euthanasia legislation warn of the hazard to vulnerable people, who, regarding themselves as a burden on the family (emotional or perhaps financial), will feel obliged to opt for euthanasia, even although they really would want to live longer. Thus, their rights may be infringed by the creation of a law which gives the right to die to those who genuinely want it, but fails to see its effect on others who wish to live.

RELIEF OF SUFFERING

For most people, it is likely that the most persuasive argument for euthanasia and PAS is that it gives people the option to die peacefully and with family and friends, without the fear of having to face unremitting pain or the indignity of institutional care. Here the key issue is whether the palliative care movement has removed the reason for such fears. As I mentioned earlier, there are a few cases in which even the skills of palliative medicine cannot alleviate the suffering fully. To deal with this, some patients have to be given what is called 'terminal sedation'. This involves using sedative drugs to render the patient unconscious (or so barely conscious that they do not feel the pain) and maintaining them in this state until they die. In this way, the pain is relieved, but the patient is not deliberately killed, since the drugs are used only to the extent necessary for relieving pain. It is around such extreme cases that the debate about what is a 'good death' is at its most acute. For some, the rational answer is to legislate for a rapid death; for others, even these exceptional cases do not justify legislation authorizing medical killing or assisting in suicide.

AFTER DEATH

In this final section I look at the ways in which the dead can still contribute to the health care of others, through the use of their bodies after death, in anatomy teaching, organ donation and the use of human tissue in research and medical products.

ANATOMICAL DISSECTION – ACKNOWLEDGING THE 'SILENT MENTORS'

The anatomical dissection of chemically preserved dead bodies (**cadavers**) is one of the hallmarks of modern, scientific medicine. For medical students (and other health professional students), it acts as a kind of transition into the secret – and at times disturbing – world of medicine. Centuries ago, the advent of scientific dissection of the dead helped to dispel false theories about the structure and function of the human body, and it also provided fascinating material for artists like Leonardo da Vinci, who spent many hours both dissecting and observing it being done. However, the history of dissection is a murky one, since for centuries it was disapproved of by the religious authorities and was used as a particularly degrading way of dealing with the bodies of criminals, adding to their punishment by the 'mutilation' of their remains. At the same time, a growing demand for cadavers, as medical education became more scientific, led to the 'resurrectionists' – entrepreneurs who stole bodies from fresh graves to sell to medical schools – and also to the notorious Edinburgh murderers, Burke and Hare, who found an even quicker and more effective way of meeting the demand by murdering the homeless! In modern times, opposition to this use of dead bodies continues in some cultures and some religions, for example, in Shintoism in Japan; and, as the number of medical schools worldwide has increased dramatically, supply through donations often does not meet demand. As a result, some medical schools have done away entirely with the use of cadavers, depending instead on computer models and other simulations, while others have to rely on unclaimed bodies, rather than on voluntary donations, to meet the educational need.

However, whatever the source of the cadavers, in those medical schools where anatomical dissection continues there is renewed emphasis on expressions of respect and gratitude to these 'silent mentors'. Campaigns to increase donations have been dramatically successful in some countries, notably Taiwan and Korea. The usefulness of dissection is seen to be more than simply learning detailed anatomy: it also gives students 'hands on' experience of dealing with bodies, and can help to develop professional attitudes to the living and the dead. Most medical schools now require their students to take an oath pledging respectful treatment of the bodies, and many have introduced closing ceremonies, led by the students, in which gratitude to the dead for their contribution to learning can be expressed in poetry and music.

GIFTS FROM THE DEAD

Apart from the contribution to medical education of these silent mentors, the dead can also help the living in more direct ways, through the use of their organs and other bodily materials for both treatment and research. We saw earlier the huge problem of the shortage of organs for transplantation. In some instances, such as heart transplantation, obviously only dead donors can be used, but organs from the deceased are also very effective in the transplantation of kidneys and other organs (though the success rate may be a little lower than from living donors). But deceased organ donation raises two major ethical issues. First, if the organs are to be useful, they must continue to be perfused with blood until as close as possible to the time of transplantation into the recipient. This requirement has led to a revision of the definition of death from the traditional one of cessation of breathing and circulation to 'brain death', the irreversible destruction of those parts of the brain which are necessary to sustain human life. This redefinition allows for what have been described as 'heart beat cadavers', donors who are legally dead, yet still have their circulation maintained by artificial means. Not all legal systems allow for such a definition, and, for those that do, the reliability of the diagnosis of death is, of course, crucial. Although the tests to be used and the procedures to be followed (such as a clear separation between the transplant team and the doctors establishing brain death) are internationally recognized, for some families and some cultures, such as Orthodox Judaism and some segments of the Japanese society, the conviction remains that such people are 'not really dead', and so deceased donation is rejected.

This leads to the second ethical issue: the nature of the consent for such donations. Here a distinction is made between 'opt in' and 'opt out' systems. In the former, there has to be clear evidence that the donor had consented to this prior to death (for example, by ticking a box on a driver's licence application form or carrying a donor card). But in the 'opt out' system consent is assumed unless the potential donor has registered an objection. Countries vary greatly in which system is used, but, interestingly, having an 'opt out' system does not in itself ensure a higher rate of deceased donations. It has been shown that other factors, mainly the way the family of the deceased is approached (whether or not they have the right to refuse consent) and the efficiency of the organization for sourcing organs, are much more important in increasing donation rates. Thus, it can be argued that the morally preferable way is one that respects the autonomy of the deceased by using only those organs which have been explicitly donated. In this way, the 'gifts from the dead' are genuine gifts. But critics of this view can of course argue that it is wrong to put the rights of the dead above those of the living!

THE BODY BAZAAR

There is, moreover, a darker side to the sourcing of materials from dead bodies, as is well documented by the book *Body Bazaar* (Andrews and Nelkin, 2001). Body parts have become big business. For example, Michael Mastromarino, a former dentist who owned a New Jersey-based firm called Biomedical Tissue Services, was convicted in 2008 in a New York Court for conspiring with funeral directors in several states to strip the body parts of corpses awaiting burial or cremation, including arm and leg bones, skin and (possibly) heart valves and veins. The products were then sold on to companies providing materials for dental implants, bone implants, skin grafts and many other medical procedures. It emerged that more than one thousand corpses had been 'harvested' in this way. This case is, of course, an extreme example of the 'body bazaar', but even where commercial gain and fraud do not enter in, medical institutions contain huge collections of human tissue and organs, often taken without the knowledge or consent of the patients or their families. For example, in the UK a major controversy erupted when it was revealed that children's organs and body parts, including hearts, brains, tongues and eyes, had been retained after post mortem examination, most of which had simply been stored and not used in any form of treatment or research (see Campbell, 2009, 96–103).

What is the alternative to these abuses of the dead and their families? Obviously, comprehensive, but not over-restrictive, legislation is needed to ensure that proper consent is obtained for removing, storing and using bodily materials, without impeding the progress of life-saving medical research. But, beyond this, the emergence of what has been called the 'tissue economy' (Waldby and Mitchell, 2006) means that we need some kind of international consensus on the appropriate use of human material. The commercial interests are so great that serious moral hazards will continue to dog the use of human organs and tissue. One idea is to define a **'bio-commons'**, so that any donated material, given proper consent, becomes available to all those working to improve human health care and does not become subject to market pressures or to the limitations of individual ownership. I shall explore this idea more fully in the next chapter, when I discuss the research resources known as **biobanks**. The essential ethical issue is how we can be sure that we honour the dead in whatever we do with their bodies.

CONCLUSIONS

It will be obvious from the length and complexity of this chapter that clinical ethics is probably the most diverse and controversial area in bioethics. From before birth until after death, there are areas of lively ethical debate, involving both rival moral theories and different cultural and religious attitudes. This has been a brief survey of the main issues, and readers may wish to explore in more detail some of the controversies in this area. Discussion in groups of some of the questions raised can be a good way of going more deeply into the issues. This discussion can focus on questions such as: Is the embryo a person? Should we allow designer babies? Is a market in human organs ethical? Should we try to prevent people from killing themselves? Is it right to lock up people with mental illness? Is letting die the same as killing? Do we have any right to say what happens to our bodies after death? To aid in this process, the suggested readings include some collections of case studies, as these can help to focus the discussion and debate.

FURTHER READING AND RESOURCES

This aspect of bioethics has by far the largest literature, and new books are constantly appearing. For a short and clear introduction to the basic requirements in both medical ethics and medical law see Tony Hope, Julian Savulescu and Judith Hendrick, *Medical Ethics and Law: The Core Curriculum* (2008). This book is based on the core curriculum used in British medical schools and is a very useful resource for quick reference to the major topics. A longer treatment of the same range of issues will be found in A. Campbell, G. Gillett and G. Jones, *Medical Ethics* (2006). The second edition of *Principles of Health Care Ethics*, edited by Ashcroft, Dawson, Draper et al., also covers this range of issues. For a source of cases for discussion in medical ethics you can refer to the Georgetown University website (http://bioethics.georgetown.edu/publications/scopenotes/sn38.htm) for access to a range of case material. There are also regular case discussions in the medical ethics journals, notably the *Hastings Center Report*, the *Journal of Medical Ethics*, the *American Journal of Bioethics* and the *Journal of Clinical Ethics*.

RESEARCH

Without properly conducted scientific research the whole enterprise of bioethics would be a waste of time. If medicine and other disciplines which affect human health and welfare were based merely on prejudice, unquestioned assumptions or reliance on past ways of practising, then what would be the point in exploring the ethical aspects? Bad science is bad ethics, and we need to be sure that what we are discussing is not mere dogma or superstition *before* we ask questions about its ethical worth or validity. Yet, as we saw in Chapter 1, research itself can be unethical, allowing the sort of gross violations of human rights that were revealed at Nuremberg and elsewhere; and there is another problem – some research may be asking the wrong questions. The methods used to achieve what has been called 'evidence-based medicine' may actually miss exploring some aspects of biomedical science that are crucial to our well-being. (For example, we may put all our effort into producing more and more pharmaceuticals – 'a pill for every ill' – when some of the real problems, like appropriate care of the dying, need quite different solutions.) As the psychologist Abraham Maslow wrote, 'I suppose it is tempting, if the only tool you have is a hammer, to treat everything as if it were a nail' (Maslow, 1966).

So, in this chapter I shall start by looking at how biomedical research has come to be regulated, in response to the major scandals revealed after the Second World War; then, I shall look at a different ethical topic, the honesty, or lack of it, by scientists when conducting and publishing the results of research – what is called 'research integrity'; and, lastly, by looking at 'research and the future', I shall consider whether, with the huge expansion of biomedical research, we have, in fact, got our priorities right.

RESEARCH ETHICS

The ethical regulation of biomedical research has arisen from an increasing awareness that researchers themselves and the funders of research (whether private or governmental) have frequently failed to see the risks to the participants (who are often patients, or others in some kind of dependent relationship to the researcher). In Chapter 1, we saw extreme examples of this – the Nazi and Japanese doctors' war-time experiments, and US government-funded research, like the Tuskegee Syphilis Study – but there have been many other examples subsequent to these early abuses, and many cases may still come to light. As a result of these scandals, there is now worldwide agreement that all research involving human subjects must be independently reviewed according to a set of international norms. Documents spelling out these norms have been produced by the World Medical Association (the Declaration of Helsinki, which has gone through many revisions), by the Council for International Organisations of Medical Sciences and the WHO, and by the US government (the Belmont Report and the Common Rule on Protection of Human Subjects). Although these codes and declarations differ in some details, they all agree on the basic requirements. These are: *protection of the research participant as paramount*; *independent ethical review*; *scientific validity of the research*; *fully informed and voluntary consent*; and an *acceptable balance of risks and benefits*.

PROTECTION AS PARAMOUNT

The Nazi doctors froze some of their victims to death and starved others of oxygen; Japanese doctors infected prisoners with fatal diseases; American doctors failed to treat their patients with the known cure for syphilis; army doctors in several countries deliberately exposed troops to radiation; cancer researchers in a terminal care hospital injected dying patients with live cancer cells to see if their bodies rejected them – and there have been many other examples of a total failure to protect the lives and health of the unwitting participants in research. That is why the Helsinki Declaration is insistent on the basic principle underlying all medical research: 'the well-being of the individual research subject must take precedence over all other interests' (World Medical Association, 2008, para. 6). Extreme examples of disregard for research participants may be rare now, but it is still not unusual for scientific enthusiasm to mask the awareness of the researcher about what will actually be involved in participating in research (for example, psychological stresses in some investigations involving whole body scanning may not be recognized); and consent may not be genuine, such as when researchers use natural disasters to conduct research under the guise of 'treatment' or with food as an inducement to participate. For this reason, independent review of the research protocol is essential.

INDEPENDENT REVIEW

The Helsinki Declaration requires that all research protocols must be submitted to a 'research ethics committee before the study begins. This committee must be independent of the researcher, the sponsor and any other undue influence' (World Medical Association, 2008, para. 15). In the USA, these ethical review committees are called Institutional Review Boards (IRBs); elsewhere they may be called Research Ethics Committees, or have other similar titles. A key issue is the independence of the committees. Since IRBs are sometimes appointed by hospitals or other institutions involved in research, it can be difficult to maintain independence and avoid conflicts of interest, and the advent of privately funded 'for profit' IRBs in the USA and elsewhere raises the question of independence even more strongly (since they may want to attract customers by not being too stringent in their requirements). Some countries (like the UK) make their ethics committees part of the regional or local organization of health services, with their authority extending over a range of providers of health care and health research. This may prevent undue influence on the committee, but another problem is getting the balance right between professional expertise and lay involvement. In some committees the lay members may be heavily outnumbered, and perhaps feel overawed by the scientific and medical members; on the other hand, a committee dominated by lay concerns may fail to understand fully some of the scientific aspects of the protocol. Other contentious issues are the ways in which members are recruited and trained, and the problem of maintaining consistency and quality of assessment across the range of committees considering the protocol. In low- and middle-income countries especially, where, increasingly, medical research is being promoted by pharmaceutical companies and other major research funders in the higher-income countries, there is a huge problem in ensuring adequate research ethics review. (I shall return to this problem later in the chapter.)

SCIENTIFIC WORTH AND VALIDITY

As I pointed out at the beginning of this chapter, poor science makes poor ethics, so a basic ethical principle is that people should not have to undergo research if it is scientifically flawed. Research Ethics Committees are not usually qualified to assess the science of the protocols, but they have to ensure that every project has scientific validity, and often members of the committee have enough expertise to see problems and so to require a proper review of the science. However, one of the other problems in assessing scientific quality is that some health research may be of a qualitative kind (using interviews or focus groups) and the scientific members of the committee are usually more accustomed to the quantitative methods of 'hard' science. Thus, fairness in the scientific assessment has to be ensured by referring to the appropriate expert reviewers.

A different set of problems arises in judging the *worth* of the research – will it genuinely gain new and beneficial knowledge? This can be seen most acutely in the huge numbers of research protocols designed to test pharmaceuticals. Some research may be simply designed to produce so-called 'me too' drugs, which are identical in nearly every respect to a currently marketed drug but have only a slight variation so as to circumvent a patent on the current one. Here the motive for the research is clearly a purely commercial one, so should an ethics committee endorse this use of patients as research subjects? (This is one of the several problems in clinical trials, to which I shall return later.) The issue of worth also arises in research which seems to be solely theoretical, with no obvious practical applications. Again, committees may be concerned about involving people in such research, especially if they are in a vulnerable situation, such as in hospital – yet, without such 'blue skies' research science cannot progress, and it could in the future yield important new treatments.

CONSENT

Some of the problems about the justification of research can be helped by ensuring that potential subjects are fully informed and are genuinely free to make up their own minds about whether to take part. We saw in Chapter 4 how important fully informed consent is in the case of medical treatment, but it is even more important in research, since, unlike treatment, there is no definite benefit to the person taking part. (Often, however, research participants wrongly believe that it will be beneficial, even when they are told that there can be no guarantee of benefit – this is known as the **'therapeutic misconception'**.) The Nuremberg Code stated that consent must be gained in *all* experimentation with human beings: 'The voluntary consent of the human subject is absolutely essential' (Nuremberg Code, clause 1). But, if this were rigorously applied, whole areas of health research would be impossible, for example, research involving young children, people with cognitive impairments, or people needing emergency treatment. In the light of this, we need to make a distinction between competent and non-competent subjects, as we do in the case of treatment. However, we cannot use the 'best interests' criterion for research, since, as already noted, in most cases there is no obvious benefit to the research subject. Instead other criteria need to be used: firstly, that the risk to the subject is 'minimal' (of course, defining what this means can be difficult!); and, secondly, that the research should be of potential benefit to that patient group (for example, research on children should be for improving paediatric care and treatment). In the case of competent subjects, very close attention has to be paid to the information given to them, and this is often a major role of Research Ethics Committees. Very frequently, information sheets are couched in technical language that no lay person could possibly understand, and often the risks or discomforts of the research are glossed over. Another problem in gaining genuine consent is that the subjects may be in a dependent relationship to the researcher (for example, a patient–doctor relationship or a student–teacher one). Again, it is the task of the ethics committee to make sure that potential research participants feel free to refuse, or to withdraw at any time from the research, and this is best assured by avoiding role conflicts (like that of doctor and patient) by requiring that consent is taken by an independent party.

BALANCE OF RISK AND BENEFIT

Since fully informed and free consent is often very difficult to ensure in research, there is a strong responsibility on ethics committee to assess fully the balance of risks and benefits in every research protocol. We saw already that direct benefits to the individual research subject are unlikely. Even if the research is trying out a potentially better treatment, the individual may be in a group that does not receive this treatment; or, if the individual is in the treatment group, it may turn out that the alternative treatment is in fact the better one. Benefit, then, can only be that of a future improvement in health care, which, of course, might then be offered to the research participants. However, there have been many examples of research (for example, drugs to treat HIV/AIDS) in which the trial participants have been unable to benefit even in the future, since they, or their country, are too poor to afford the medication. For this reason, ethics committees need to look very critically at whether there is any sharing of benefits, either with individual participants or with the community from which they come. The Helsinki Declaration makes this clear: 'Medical research involving a disadvantaged or vulnerable population or community is only justified if the research is responsive to the health needs and priorities of this population or community and if there is a reasonable likelihood that this population or community stands to benefit from the results of the research' (World Medical Association, 2008, clause 17).

So far as risks are concerned, these have to be assessed for both severity and probability, and must include both physical and psychological risk. In the case of pharmaceuticals, there has to be a set of trial phases, including animal studies and trials on healthy volunteers, before they can be tested on patients. In all research, the protection of the research participant remains paramount, and so, if an ethics committee foresees any serious risk from the research, it cannot be authorized, even though that risk might be fully described in the information sheet and informed consent is obtained from the participants.

TYPES OF RESEARCH

These general principles apply across the whole range of research with human beings, but there are also some specific issues in particular types of research. I shall consider four different areas: clinical trials; the use of animals in medical research; genetic research; and epidemiological research.

CLINICAL TRIALS

A clinical trial (which is usually of a drug, but could also be of other types of treatment or of medical devices) involves the use of patients as research subjects and normally employs the classic research method known as the *randomized clinical trial* (RCT). In the standard RCT, patients are randomly allocated to a *control group* and an *experimental group*. The control group may be given the standard treatment for their disease or they may be given a *placebo* (a dummy drug), while the experimental group is given the product to be tested. In what is called a *double blind* RCT neither the researcher nor the research subject knows which group any patient is assigned to. (This can later be found out by consulting the coding system used to assign patients to groups.) This method is thought to be the most likely to produce scientifically valid results, since it seeks to eliminate any bias coming from the knowledge of patients or researchers about what treatment is being given, but it does raise separate ethical issues. The most obvious one is that, if a placebo is used, the patient may be placed at unacceptable risk by being taken off their current medication; if alternative treatments are used, then the researchers should be genuinely uncertain of the comparative effectiveness of the medication being trialled (this is known as 'clinical equipoise'), but it is often difficult to be sure that this uncertainty exists. A third area of concern, noted earlier, is that trials of pharmaceuticals may be driven as much by commercial considerations as by the likelihood of real therapeutic gain. Related to this problem is evidence that the pharmaceutical industry has used many strategies for drawing its particular product to the attention of doctors, for example by sponsoring tourist trips and expensive meals for those attending conferences where the product is being promoted. Enlisting doctors as researchers can be seen as a very effective way of ensuring that they also become regular prescribers of a particular brand. Thus, the whole question of the *worth* of the research must be constantly revisited, and unethical inducements (like paying doctors for the number of patients they recruit into a trial, and excessive payments to participants) must be prohibited. This is a problem to which I return later in the chapter, when I look at the problem of skewed priorities in health research.

THE USE OF ANIMALS

Another very contentious area in biomedical research is the use of animals to determine the safety and effectiveness of products before trials are begun on human subjects. Some ethics scholars (of whom the best known is Peter Singer – see his book, *Animal Liberation*) believe that we have no moral right to treat animals merely as means to our own ends. Singer calls this 'speciesism', and he equates it with racism, sexism and other ways of treating others in unjustifiably discriminatory ways. The debate here evokes some of the ethical theories and perspectives discussed in previous chapters. For example, the reverence for all life found in Buddhism would see animals to be as worthy of respect and compassion as any other living creatures; and a utilitarian calculus of happiness can see the suffering of animals as wholly relevant to the need to maximize happiness and minimize pain in this world (Jeremy Bentham said of animals, 'The question is not, Can they *reason*? Nor can they *talk*?, but can they *suffer*?' (Bentham, 1879, original italics)). On the other hand, if we base our morality on the concept of rational moral agency (as Kant does) or on the achievement of *human* fulfilment (as in VE), then animals are not going to be seen as of an equal moral status to humans, though their suffering should be kept to a minimum.

An alternative view on the use of animals, called the welfarist approach, seeks to minimize both the suffering inflicted on animals in medical research and the number of animals used (and normally subsequently killed). Most international legislation on animal research stems from this outlook, and is based on the 'four Rs' in animal use: **R**espect (at all stages animals should be treated with their welfare in mind); **R**eduction (the total number of animals used should be kept to a minimum); **R**efinement (experimental techniques should be refined to ensure the minimization or elimination of pain and distress); and **R**eplacement (a consistent search for different models to do the research, for example, computer-based programmes that model effects on humans, or the use of animals that are less likely to experience pain and distress than the higher vertebrates). In many countries, experiments using animals are supervised by specialized ethics committees which will operate according to these principles. However, for those who advocate animal liberation, none of these measures is sufficient. They argue strongly that animals provide poor models for determining whether drugs and other products are safe and effective for human use, and that, even if they were, we should never treat non-human animals as though they had no rights to life and freedom. (To be consistent, this view must, of course, also oppose the use of animals for transportation, entertainment, sport and food.)

GENETIC RESEARCH

Genetic research raises some special issues, due partly to the fact that genetic information relates not just to the person whose genes are studied, but also to the family as a whole and to its forebears and descendants. Another factor which seems to make genetic research special is that many people put a heavy emphasis on the importance of genetically based predictions of disease, not realizing that nearly all diseases or illnesses result from a combination of genetic and environmental causes, and that often the most important factor is the environment or the life style of the person. (So, for example, whether a predisposition to heart disease will result in a person becoming ill depends very heavily on other factors such as smoking, diet, exercise and stress.) Because of this mistaken over-emphasis on genetic factors, genetic tests can often be harmful to the person in terms of their prospects for health insurance or for employment. There is also the risk that genetic studies may reveal unwanted information, for example, about paternity or incest. Finally, poor genetic research can result in the stigmatization of a whole ethnic group. A clear example of this was the claim by a researcher to have discovered a 'warrior gene', which would predispose the Maori population of New Zealand towards higher levels of violence (Yong, 2010). This claim resulted in reinforcing stereotypes of a whole ethnic group, yet such a major and wide-ranging conclusion was certainly not established by the research.

For all these reasons, special attention has to be paid to the interpretation and control of genetic information. Before the research begins, several policies have to be established: (1) Should family members always be informed about findings relevant to them, and how can we find out if this is what they would want? (2) What results should be fed back to research participants? (3) Who will determine the criteria for clinical significance, and is it right to pass on information about a condition for which there is no prevention or cure? (4) How will the confidentiality of the information be safeguarded, so that research participants do not suffer from discrimination in insurance or employment? (5) How will false generalizations from genetic studies of specific groups be avoided, especially if the media are involved in reporting them? If all of these issues are adequately dealt with at the outset of the research, then it may be possible to avoid what has been called 'genetic exceptionalism', that is, giving credence to the idea that 'it's all in our genes', when in fact much of our health and well-being depends on how we conduct our lives and on how our social circumstances promote or threaten our welfare.

EPIDEMIOLOGICAL RESEARCH

Health data have a wider significance than simply the health of the person from whom test results and medical and family history are obtained. Epidemiological research depends on seeing associations between large banks of data gathered over extended periods of time. Famous examples of this are: (1) the research which showed that smoking was both highly addictive and the cause of a whole range of major disorders; and (2) the association discovered between the pollution caused by lead in petrol and a reduction in children's cognitive ability, which resulted in the development of unleaded petrol. Such epidemiological research depends on access to information which was initially obtained to help the treatment of individuals, and so could be protected by the requirement of medical confidentiality. Yet, it is very often quite impractical to go back to all those individuals from whom the data come (many of whom in any case may be dead) in order to seek their consent for use of the information for this purpose. It may also be impossible to make the data totally anonymous, as some of the important information needed could also result in the identification of the persons being studied. So some solution must be found if vital epidemiological research is to proceed. This may mean putting trust in the researchers not to use the information for any purpose other than getting aggregate data; another answer is to use 'trusted third parties', who code the data and provide it in this form to those who are studying the associations with other data (such as mortality statistics). By this means, no one person is able to relate all the information to any one individual.

These dilemmas in epidemiological research illustrate the general point that there are many situations in bioethics when the rights of individuals to such things as privacy and confidentiality cannot be absolute if major social benefits are at stake. We see here the tension between the extreme individualism of some theories of human rights and the demands of social solidarity or communitarianism.

RESEARCH INTEGRITY

Scientific research depends crucially on the honesty of scientists in both carrying out the research and reporting the results. As the author C. P. Snow put it, 'The only ethical principle which has made science possible is that the truth shall be told all the time' (Snow, 2000). Unfortunately, not all scientists abide by this principle, and it is likely that scientific misconduct is on the increase, as more and more pressure is applied to make scientific breakthroughs (especially those with commercial applications) and to promote one's career through publications in **high-impact journals**. A recent famous example of such dishonesty were the publications of the South Korean stem cell researcher Hwang Woo-suk. In 2004 and 2005 he published claims that he had succeeded in creating the first cloned human embryo and had derived a stem cell line from it; and later that he had established 11 'patient specific' cloned stem cell lines. These claims were subsequently shown to be totally false, since there was in fact no match between the allegedly cloned cell and the donor, and no match between the cell lines and the embryos from which they were said to be derived. Other major examples of scientific fraud have been revealed. One American scientist, W. T. Summerlin, claimed that he had grafted tissue from one (black) mouse onto a white one, when in fact he had produced the black markings using a felt-tipped pen (Brody, 1974)! In another example a British gynaecologist, Malcolm Pearce, reported the successful re-implantation of an ectopic pregnancy (in which the embryo has not implanted in the woman's womb) and a subsequent live birth; and also claimed to have carried out a trial of 200 women, sponsored by a pharmaceutical company, of a drug for dealing with polycystic ovary syndrome. However, it emerged that there had never been the case of successful implantation that he described, nor had the drug trial taken place. (In fact, the 'sponsoring pharmaceutical company' did not exist!). Such cases are extreme examples of fraud, but surveys of scientists have indicated that various forms of research misconduct are not uncommon.

We can identify several different forms of misconduct in research. These are: *fabrication* of data; *falsification* of data; copying another person's work without acknowledgment (*plagiarism*); and *false claims to authorship*. There are also ethical problems associated with communicating scientific findings to the public media.

FABRICATION

Sometimes researchers have simply invented data to 'prove' their hypothesis. Data might be inserted into a chart or table that had not been found in the experiments conducted. In extreme cases, there could be claims to research findings where no experiment had been conducted at all (such as the mouse marked with a felt-tipped pen).

FALSIFICATION

In this case, images or data are manipulated to fit a theory, or data are excluded that contradict the hypothesis. Falsification can also be achieved by employing deliberately inadequate or misleading statistical analyses. Another version of falsification consists in altering the numbers in a calculation to make the hypothesis more convincing, with no justification from the research findings for such numbers.

PLAGIARISM

Plagiarism consists in presenting another person's ideas as though they were your own. Sections of another person's work (whether published or unpublished) can be pasted into an article or research report, with no acknowledgment of the source, and so there is the implicit claim that it is one's own original work. Sometimes plagiarism is carried out by stealing ideas from research proposals or from manuscripts submitted for publication, so that dishonest reviewers of the proposal or the submitted paper can get 'a head start' and claim the work as original to themselves.

FALSE CLAIMS TO AUTHORSHIP

Finally, scientific misconduct can consist of requiring, or allowing, one's name to appear as an author when in fact the work was entirely done by others, with the claimed author having no part in the preparation, the drafting or the subsequent final editing of the piece. This is not uncommon in situations where a senior figure heads up a research project and insists on being an author in all papers, even when all the work and writing up has been done by junior members of the team. Honesty in this context requires that the proportion of input of all the claimed authors to the article be clearly stated – and many scientific journals now require this. Another example of fraudulent authorship is 'ghost writing' and 'gift authorship'. In this case a sponsor, such as a health-product company, wishes to use the name of a prestigious figure in the field as an author so as to give credence to the product, when, in fact, the whole article has been written by the sponsor. (The recipient of this 'gift authorship' also benefits from this arrangement by adding to his or her publication list without doing any work!)

MEDIA HYPE

Another problem related to the communication of results is the temptation to 'hype' scientific findings by releasing exaggerated claims to the public media. This was clearly an element in the Hwang cloning scandal, in which the South Korean authorities tried to raise national prestige by worldwide publicity about the alleged breakthrough and to make the researcher into a national hero – until, of course, the falsity of his claims was revealed! Earlier, we saw how the media accounts of a 'warrior gene' (whether or not this term was endorsed by the researcher) led to a public outcry about racism. A similar situation arose in the hugely politically contentious area of climate change. Attempts were made to discredit scientific findings about human causation of global warming by publishing e-mail correspondence between scientists in which the uncertainty of some data was discussed (BBC, 2009c). Such openness to the possible falsification of a hypothesis is an essential part of the scientific approach but, in this case, it was used to claim that the scientists were deliberately misleading the public (even though the cumulative evidence for the hypothesis that humans are the main creators of global warming is overwhelming). All these examples show that scientific integrity depends not only on the way in which the research is conducted and published in scientific journals, but also on the accuracy and honesty of any media reporting. Science can retain its integrity only if its findings are not distorted, exaggerated or manipulated for personal or political gain. Humility and caution may be good virtues for scientists to cultivate!

There is increasing concern in the scientific community worldwide about all these examples of misconduct, since they undercut drastically the veracity of scientific claims. Increasingly, institutions are adopting procedures to deal with scientific fraud (including measures to protect whistle blowers, and compulsory courses in scientific integrity). In the USA, a federal agency has been set up to investigate and, if need be, penalize those perpetrating such misconduct. The Office of Research Integrity is sponsored by the

US Public Health Service and its procedures can be found on its website (http://ori.hhs.gov/statutes-regulations). In the last analysis, however, only the honesty of the scientists themselves can be an effective barrier against research misconduct. Whether we see this as a matter of expediency, duty or virtue, true science can survive and prosper only when the vast majority of scientists are willing to protect and exemplify its fundamental value: the disinterested pursuit of reliable knowledge, based solely on experimental evidence.

RESEARCH AND THE FUTURE

So what can we expect from biomedical research in the future? We probably need to distinguish between what we hope for (what *ought* to happen) and what may be the more likely future trends in research (what *probably will* happen). We would surely all hope that biomedical research would rid itself of fraud, dishonesty and the mere pursuit of commercial gain irrespective of benefit to health; and that it would enhance human health and welfare globally, helping to overcome some of the gross disparities in health between the rich and the poor nations of the world. (I shall be describing these disparities in more detail in the next chapter.) Yet, what seems more likely to happen is that dreams of perfect health by the better-off will determine the research agenda, and that the dominance of health research by the medical-device and pharmaceutical industries will increase, ensuring ever more expensive health care interventions which overlook the health problems of most of the world's population. So which is dream and which is future reality? I shall consider, first, the claims about human enhancement, which see a utopian 'posthuman' future just over the horizon; and then look at alternatives aimed at directing research, through international collaboration, towards the main health challenges facing humankind.

FUTURE PERFECT?

Developments in modern biomedicine have raised the possibility of making people 'better than well', changing the focus from the overcoming of disease to the enhancement of our normal human capacities. For example, the skills of plastic and reconstructive surgery, honed by the need to deal with the horrific injuries of war and road traffic accidents, have been transformed into 'cosmetic' or 'aesthetic' surgery, a hugely profitable area of medical practice, in which people's bodies are shaped or 'sculpted' into what are seen by the consumers of these services as 'better' forms. Equally, drugs developed for disabling conditions such as attention deficit disorder in young children or clinical depression can now be used for improved concentration when studying for examinations or for giving one a constantly 'happy' mood – the so-called Prozac revolution, foreseen by the novelist Aldous Huxley in *Brave New World*. Moreover, as national and international sports events have become increasingly competitive and financially lucrative, an array of drugs originally developed to treat medical conditions have been used to enhance athletic performance, leading to major concerns about unfairness and the demise of the sporting spirit.

These constantly expanding possibilities for human enhancement can be divided into several categories: (1) *physical enhancement* (surgical or medical interventions which change both bodily appearance and physical capacities for strength, endurance and speed); (2) *lifespan extension* (drugs counteracting the physical and mental effects of aging, possibly enabling people to live for centuries rather than decades); (3) *cognitive enhancement* (increasing the mental capacities of attention, memory and possibly even reasoning power); (4) *mood enhancement* (reducing or eliminating altogether feelings of grief, shyness, low self-esteem and depression); and (5) *moral enhancement* (using drugs or genetic manipulation to make people more altruistic and less aggressive). At the extreme end of this quest for human perfectibility is the transhumanist movement, which looks towards a 'posthuman' future, when humans will have perfected their physical and mental abilities with the aid of nanotechnology and artificial intelligence, creating a perfectly engineered world of human contentment. (Some proponents of this view foresee an eternal survival of the individual, even after death of the body, through downloading one's mind or personality onto a computer.)

Numerous criticisms have been made of these transhumanist claims, which can be described as inhabiting a borderline world between justifiable scientific prediction and the futuristic projections of science fiction. Firstly, critics have pointed out that the current evidence for effective enhancement of human capacities is very sparse. This is especially true of cognitive enhancement, in which the actual gains in memory and reasoning have been shown to be minimal or even absent, despite the widespread notion that they can be used to improve intellectual performance. There are also questions about whether making people more content, or less aggressive, or more altruistic, by means of drugs is in any sense a moral gain, since these states of mind, rather than being authentic commitments of the person, are simply a form of chemical coercion. Another area of debate comes from the term 'enhancement' itself. In what sense of 'better' are these changes to human capacities or to the human lifespan a genuine improvement on the current human state? Why would we want such a 'posthuman' future? Are our lives better if we become physically stronger or more agile, or have an increased intelligence, or live for centuries? Such claims appear to depend upon unquestioned value assumptions about what is worthwhile in human life.

The debate about what constitutes a morally good human life is likely to continue indefinitely, and, of course, it hinges around the different moral theories we discussed in Chapter 2. Transhumanism may find more support in Greatest Happiness and libertarian theories than it does in theories which stress moral agency or the pursuit of the virtuous life. But even while this debate rages on, a still more critical question can be raised about this focus on attempts to enhance humans: why should we be putting resources into this kind of research – which can surely only benefit a privileged minority in rich countries – when so many human beings are still unable to receive the most basic means of survival and are prone to diseases for which there is already a known cure? It seems that we may be getting our research priorities disastrously wrong.

RESEARCH PRIORITIES: THE 10/90 GAP

In 1996 the WHO Ad Hoc Committee on Health Research reported a '10/90 gap', signifying that less than 10 per cent of the billions of dollars spent on health research is devoted to the health problems which account for 90 per cent of the global disease burden; moreover, most of this disease burden is borne by poor nations least likely to benefit from most international research.

There are several factors contributing to this massive gap. The first is the nature of the commercial priorities in the pharmaceutical industry, which are designed to maximize the return to shareholders, rather than to produce an effective range of drugs of relevance to the health needs of the world as a whole. As we saw earlier, this means that there is a focus on 'me too' drugs, close analogues to existing medications, designed to ensure new patent protection. There is nothing obviously ethically unacceptable in this business plan, since these are private enterprises whose purpose is to maximize profit within ethical and legal boundaries, not to deal with health inequities. However, other aspects of international research raise questions about its ethical status. The first is the outsourcing of research to low- or middle-income countries that are unlikely to benefit from the results of the research. Currently, just under half (43 per cent) of clinical trials sponsored by US pharmaceutical companies take place outside that country; yet these companies control the agenda for research, determining which countries and institutions will gain any benefit and controlling the subsequent publication of results and pricing and distribution of the product. Second, the conduct of research is being increasingly streamlined, through the use of Contract Research Organizations (CROs). In a one-window operation, CROs manage all aspects of clinical trials, including developing protocols, obtaining ethics approval from for-profit review boards, recruiting subjects through incentives to physicians and hospitals and analysing data. The activities of these CROs are hard to both monitor and regulate, since they cross so many national boundaries. Third, increased regulation of human-subject research in wealthy countries is driving the industry to outsource clinical drug trials to developing countries with large pools of impoverished, uneducated people, vulnerable populations that are too poor to afford medications, unaware of their rights and with little or no defence against exploitation by researchers. This problem is especially severe in countries where medical incomes are very low and doctors depend on making a reasonable income both by 'under the counter' payments from patients or their families and by large payments from research sponsors for conducting trials. For all these reasons, there is much less health benefit from the massive expenditure on health research than could be achieved if the priorities in research projects were aligned to the needs of the majority of the world's population.

Is it possible to see a more ethical approach to this problem than the current, market-driven prioritization? Some solutions may be found in legislation and regulation. International agreements on trade and national policies on health research could be amended to prevent at least some of the major examples of exploitation and corruption. Other solutions have been suggested whereby market forces would be used to change research priorities. One way would be to set up a prize fund which would be used to give a major financial reward to individuals, groups or companies who find effective and inexpensive solutions to neglected global health problems; another (developed by the philosopher Thomas Pogge) would be to set up a health impact fund. Such a fund would do away with patents (and so keep prices down), and reward companies on the basis of the health impact of their new products. Such solutions have recently been assessed by an expert panel set up by the WHO (Consultative Expert Working Group on Research and Development: Financing and Coordination, 2012), and it is likely that international efforts will be made to implement some of them, if the individual nations that are members of the WHO are willing to raise the necessary revenue.

Another way of reducing the 10/90 gap would be a change in attitudes towards the sharing of publicly funded scientific discoveries. (To the extent that many private research enterprises also benefit from direct or indirect government subsidies, this could also change their practices.) Increasingly, scientists and their funders are viewing scientific discovery as part of the public sphere, not as private property protected by patents, and so open access to the data, after an interval to allow the researchers to gain credit for discovery, is being required. In this regard, health research would be promoted and protected by a communitarian ethic, which sees human solidarity and mutual benefit as a cornerstone of all such research, rather than the maximization of private profit.

One example of this change in research values can be seen in the development of biobanks. The term 'biobank' denotes a very large collection of biological samples or genetic data which can be linked to the life style and health history of those individuals from whom the samples were obtained. Thus, biobanks provide a rich resource for research projects of all sorts. In the future, they will provide much better information about the complex factors that cause disease, and also about which are the most effective and inexpensive ways of either preventing the onset of disease or providing a cure. So they have the potential to be a major weapon in the fight against the major health problems facing the world at the present time.

Biobanks do not, however, provide a quick or magical solution. It will take many years to build up the data needed, and international co-operation is essential to ensure that the information is relevant globally and available to all researchers. There are many different biobanks throughout the world (mostly in developed countries) and they vary greatly in the way they were created and the way they are governed. Some are retrospective (linking already collected samples and other data); others are prospective, recruiting volunteers who are willing to provide samples and other information and to have their health records interrogated over decades. (An example of the latter type is the UK Biobank, which successfully recruited 500,000 volunteers aged between 40 and 65 from a wide cross-section of the British population, but will make its data available internationally if it judges a research project to be of sufficient merit.)

There is a huge potential for global health research if the numerous national biobanks can be linked (with proper safeguards for confidentiality) and used for agreed research priorities related to the health problems of 90 per cent of the world's population. The metaphor of a 'commons' which must be protected from enclosure by commercial interests seems to point a way forward. In this conceptualization, human materials and the information derived from them are treated like common grazing land, rather than as fenced private property accessible only to the powerful. So biobanks would become a first step in what could be the case in the future, a shared effort to prioritize health research according to need rather than profit.

CONCLUSION

Modern medicine and health care have been transformed by biomedical research. In the era of modern, scientific medicine, there have been numerous examples of new treatments, such as antibiotic therapy, or of preventive measures, such as vaccinations, that have brought increased health and life expectancy to at least some parts of the world. But research is not a good in itself, not an intrinsic good, since it all depends both how it is carried out and what purposes it serves. For example, research that can aid in the eradication of infectious disease can also be used to spread it through biological warfare; and research into human psychology, designed to help people overcome mental illness, could also be used to create more sophisticated forms of torture. Research can be coercive and exploitative, and researchers themselves can be dishonest and self-serving. For all these reasons, bioethics has to be concerned with the ethics of both research and researchers. It has to ask critical and searching questions about the aims, methods and conduct of research. But, as we have seen in the final section, perhaps the key ethical question is whether all the effort and money expended has been put to the best uses that it could be. In the last chapter I shall look at this question as it relates to problems of worldwide justice (and maybe to the survival of the world itself). As one writer has put it, we need to be sure we are not just rearranging deckchairs on the *Titanic*, doing pointless things on a vessel that is doomed to destruction.

SUGGESTIONS FOR FURTHER READING

By far the best sources for detailed information on research ethics and research integrity are the NIH website (http://bioethics.od.nih. gov/) and the NIH Fogarty International Centre (http://www. fic.nih.gov/RESEARCHTOPICS/Pages/Bioethics.aspx). Although both based in the USA, these cover research worldwide, and all the key documents and regulations can be found there. On the history of, and some current debates in, research ethics, the best source is a reader edited by Emanuel, Crouch, Arras et al., *Ethical and Regulatory Aspects of Health Research* (2003). For a series of incisive and critical essays in the topic area, spanning several years, see Ruth Macklin, *Ethics in Global Health* (2012). For discussion of the controversies over ESCs, see *Contested Cells: Global Perspectives on the Stem Cell Debate*, edited by Benjamin Capps and Alastair Campbell (2010). A balanced discussion of the use of animals in research will be found in Ben Mepham's *Bioethics: An Introduction for the Biosciences* (2008). The debate over human enhancement and post-humanism is well covered in *Enhancing Human Capacities* (2011), edited by Julian Savulescu, Ruud ter Meulen and Guy Kahane. There is a lively discussion of the 'better than well' problem in Carl Elliott and Peter Kramer's *Better than Well: American Medicine Meets the American Dream* (2004). For the problem of the 10/90 gap in health priorities you can go to the WHO website, as well as to the NIH literature resources.

JUSTICE

INTRODUCTION

Justice is something every child seems to know about from an early age. How often do parents hear the complaint 'But that isn't *fair!*' Justice, seen as 'fairness', means that everyone should be treated equally, unless there are differences between them to justify unequal treatment. So, when children say, 'But that's not fair!' they might be complaining about unequal shares of a treat, or, perhaps, being made to go to bed earlier than other children of the same age. Of course, these are trivial examples, but questions of equal treatment and fair shares are very serious in the adult world, and relate not only to shares of material resources, such as food and water, or land, or income, but also to equality in the possession of basic human rights – freedom from unjustified criminal proceedings, such as unlawful arrest and detention, the right to vote and to be given equal opportunities for participation in society, and fair access to education, employment and health care.

We can distinguish between different spheres of justice: *criminal justice*, which ensures fairness and impartiality in defining and dealing with crimes and in punishing offenders; *civil justice*, which arbitrates in disputes between people or institutions on such matters as finance, property and contracts; *social justice*, which seeks a balance between the rights of the individual and the welfare of society as a whole; and *distributive justice*, which deals with the fair distribution of burdens and benefits in society. In this chapter I will be looking at only the last two types, social justice and distributive justice, as these relate to the area of bioethics. So, first, I shall look at the dilemmas of public health ethics, where we need to balance the good of society with the freedom of the individual, then I shall discuss three key issues in distributive justice in bioethics: access to health care; global inequities in health; and global survival.

PUBLIC HEALTH ETHICS

We can date public health ethics back to nineteenth-century England, when massive outbreaks of cholera were decimating the population and causing fear and alarm in all the major cities, most especially London. The popular medical theory of the time was that the disease was caused by 'bad air' or a 'noxious miasma'. In fact, cholera is spread by insanitary conditions and, in particular, contaminated drinking water. This was clearly established by a physician, John Snow, who discovered that the highest incidence of the disease in the Soho district of London was in an area round the water pump in Broad Street. Snow was able to halt the spread of the disease by the simple expedient of having the handle of the pump removed!

This combination of the scientific study of patterns of disease and its associations with other social factors (now called epidemiology), allied to decisive social action, is the concern of public health ethics. It explores the ethical aspects of the policies and programmes that can both prevent disease and promote health in the population as a whole, possibly involving restricting the freedom of individuals for the public good. We can look at two examples of this in current health and social policies. Firstly, there is the field of *preventive medicine*, which devises measures to prevent or control disease. Secondly, there is the field of *health promotion*, which uses various means to encourage healthier life styles through persuasion, education and legislation.

PREVENTIVE MEDICINE

Preventive medicine uses various measures to attempt to prevent or control the spread of disease. These are: screening; vaccination and immunization; and compulsory notification of disease and controls on the movement of infected people.

SCREENING

Screening consists in administering tests to people to see if they either have or are in danger of developing a disease, or are in danger of passing on a disease to their children. It can be done prenatally (for example, to detect whether a foetus is affected by Down syndrome or other genetic defects), postnatally (a good example is the test on newborn babies for PKU – Phenylketonuria, a rare but very serious disease), or to young people and adults (for example, to test for sexually transmitted infections, or susceptibility to breast cancer, or for the gene that would result in their children developing cystic fibrosis). The ethical problems here are to do with the accuracy of the tests and with whether they are optional or mandatory. In the case of screening for PKU, many countries and states make it compulsory for all babies, since it can be treated effectively by dietary restrictions, but will lead to severe brain damage and mental retardation if untreated. But what about tests where there could be 'false positives', meaning that the person will not in fact develop the condition, or 'false negatives', when the person is wrongly reassured that they are clear, when in fact the disease has not been detected? The problem of inaccurate predictions means that most screening should be optional, with the person (or the legal guardian) given full information about the strength of the prediction and about what, if anything, can be done if the test is positive.

VACCINATION AND IMMUNIZATION

Vaccines contain a dead or live but weakened germ that can cause a particular disease, like tetanus or smallpox. When we are given a vaccine, our body immediately produces antibodies against the foreign body. Immunization occurs when our body has developed immunity to it, either because we have been vaccinated or because we have already contracted the disease and recovered from it. Vaccination does *not* guarantee immunity. Natural immunity happens only after one has recovered from the actual disease, but for most people vaccination is a very effective way of preventing them from developing the full-blown illness, and it has resulted in a dramatic reduction in infectious diseases (at least in the wealthier nations of the world). Another important outcome of widespread vaccination is that it reduces the prevalence of the disease in whole populations (producing what is called 'herd immunity'), thus reducing the risk of anyone in that group becoming infected, even if they are not immune.

As with screening, the main ethical issue is whether there should be a mandatory or a voluntary policy for vaccinating children against the most serious and common diseases (for example measles, mumps and rubella, the three diseases prevented by the MMR vaccination). There may be some discomfort for the individual child, and, in very rare cases, possibly some serious side-effects, but if too many parents refuse to have their children vaccinated the disease will spread and herd immunity will be lost. Thus, there is a clear conflict between individual choice and community benefit. So-called 'free riders', who refuse to have their children undergo any vaccination risk, but then rely on most parents agreeing so that their own child will be protected by herd immunity, seem to lack a social conscience. Moreover, if their example is widely followed they do not in fact protect their child, since, as we have seen, herd immunity will be compromised! Despite this risk, most countries do not enforce vaccinations, but rely instead on indirect means of getting parents to comply, for example, by making it a condition of school entry.

PANDEMIC CONTROLS

Diseases do not respect national boundaries, and so the spread of serious diseases worldwide (pandemics, like the SARS outbreak) will often mean putting major restrictions on individual liberty. At the more moderate end of these controls are temperature screening and other health checks on travellers, which can result in their being refused permission to travel. At the most extreme end are measures to isolate infectious individuals, such as home quarantine or even isolation in a special facility until they are no longer a risk to others. Another measure is to compel health care practitioners to notify the authorities of the details of all affected patients (thus breaching confidentiality) so that, if need be, these people's freedom can be restricted so long as they are infectious.

In all these examples the requirements of preventive medicine illustrate the limitations of making individual autonomy the only norm in bioethics. There are clear examples of when potential harm to others will require compulsory measures to control the actions of those who may fail to act responsibly. The dilemma, however, is to know how high the likelihood of harm should be in order trigger such restrictions, and what degree of restriction on freedom is justified by it. Proportionality between harm and benefit must be maintained, so that panic over the spread of disease does not result in unfair restrictions on individuals.

HEALTH PROMOTION

The same tension between freedom and control can be seen in efforts to promote healthier behaviour in individuals and populations. An extreme example of coercion in order to achieve social goals is the 'one child' policy in the People's Republic of China. The policy prohibits certain groups (ethnic Han Chinese living in urban areas) from having more than one child, in order to slow down the population growth in the world's most highly populated nation. The policy has reduced the rate of growth, but has also resulted in an imbalance between males and females because of the social preference for boys, and it is also reported to have led to forced abortions and sterilizations, and even to infanticide. However, there are other examples, in more liberal countries, of coercive measures to achieve health goals, notably laws relating to car seat belts and to motorcycle and bicycle helmets. In these cases, restrictions on individual behaviour can be very effective in reducing the seriousness of injuries from road traffic accidents, thus saving health care costs.

In a grey area between compulsion and individual choice are uses of advertising techniques to warn people of risks to their health. Notable examples have been the Australian government's 'grim reaper' advertisements, warning people of the lethal effects of AIDS resulting from unprotected sex; and graphic images on cigarette packets (in some but by no means all countries) showing the range of diseases and disfigurements caused by smoking. Although such health promotion methods are not coercive, they do seek to change behaviour by the same kind of powerfully persuasive methods that are used to sell products (lethal or otherwise). So it could be argued that people are not given a chance to make a considered decision. But, of course, the same can be said of any effective marketing, since it rarely, if ever, appeals merely to rational choice. The founder of the Salvation Army, General Booth, is reported to have said, 'Why should the devil have all the best tunes?' and the same might be said by those trying to persuade people to protect their own health. If better health is the outcome, then maybe the methods employed are justified. Other methods of health promotion can be described as 'health education', since these rely on factual evidence and rational argument to persuade people to change their unhealthy habits. A good example of this is information on healthy and unhealthy diets and clear labelling on food packets.

We can see, then, that social justice requires that we either *persuade* or *compel* people to act for the good of all (and often at the same time also for their own good). If we want to retain the priority of liberty in ethics, then the best way of achieving this would be to create a civil society in which people were committed to the welfare of all, not just to their individual advantage (the communitarian approach described in Chapter 2). The dilemma, however, is that this may not be easily achievable, and so we may need to use the force of advertising or of the law to ensure a maximization of the public good.

FAIR ACCESS AND THE PARADOX OF HEALTH CARE

We turn now to a different realm of justice, distributive justice, in which we are concerned not with influencing people's behaviour for the common good, but with ensuring that they get a fair share of that good. On the basis of an understanding of distributive justice as fairness in the distribution of rights and benefits, we can see why discrimination in access to health care in terms of gender or sexual orientation, ethnicity, age, religion, political beliefs or social class is – on the face of it at least – unjust. (We would need to find very good reasons for showing why these differences in any way justified unequal treatment.) However, deciding what is fair is not always as easy as such blatant examples of racism or sexism might suggest. Fairness can in some circumstances mean treating people unequally. The Greek philosopher Aristotle said that 'We must treat equals equally, but unequals unequally'. Another way of putting this is to say that we should treat people in a way that is proportionate to their relevant differences. This can be described as *equitable* treatment, rather than equal treatment.

But what are the relevant differences? What kind of differences justify unequal treatment in health care? A person's age is an obvious example: we do not expect young children to be able to look after themselves properly without help; and the same may apply to very elderly people, if they lose some of their mental or physical capacities. There also are many examples where the lottery of life has given people an unequal share of ill-health, perhaps through inherited physical or mental disabilities, or as the result of catastrophic illness or accidents. These examples give us a clue about how we might understand distributive justice in health care. It will be achieved by paying attention to the wide differences in the needs and capacities of people. These differences can be seen as ethically relevant ones, possibly justifying unequal treatment; and we can go further by employing a *positive* theory of justice as fairness, which would seek not just to *meet* needs, but to *alleviate* people's needs and to *restore* or *improve* their capacities.

However, achieving fairness in the distribution of the means to health is made still harder by our uncertainty in knowing how to define health. As we noted in Chapter 1, when the WHO was founded, it adopted a highly idealistic definition of health: 'Health is a state of complete physical, mental and social well-being, not merely negatively as the absence of disease or infirmity' (World Health Organization, 1948). This definition has often been criticized because it seems impossible to achieve, yet the WHO has never changed it. Clearly, no one is likely to attain such a complete state of well-being, and many will fall very far short of it. However, it can be seen as a kind of vision to aspire to, a reminder that too-narrow a definition, for example, one which focuses on what medical treatment might achieve, can miss out other critical factors in ensuring health, such as the social and physical conditions in which people live and work. So, treating people fairly will mean not only giving them equal access to health care (though this is obviously important), but also creating and sustaining an environment in which people can flourish physically, mentally and socially.

But in trying to achieve this worthy goal of health for all, we run into another problem: modern medicine has been a victim of its own success. In higher-income countries, where infant mortality has been dramatically reduced and life expectancy has been raised well past 'three score years and ten', the costs of health care continue to spiral upwards, making it increasingly hard for individuals, insurers or governments to foot the bill. This has been called the 'paradox of health care' – if it is successful, the demand for it, instead of decreasing, continues to rise, ensuring that demand will always outstrip supply. This is due to a number of factors. Firstly, we now have the ability to extend the life expectancy of people with conditions which would have been almost immediately fatal in the past – organ transplantation provides a good example of this, and another example would be our ability to keep premature infants alive at earlier and earlier stages. This leads to raised expectations about what medicine can achieve, and so to a constantly increasing demand for highly expensive technical solutions to health problems. Secondly, as people live longer they become prone to a wide range of chronic diseases which are not open to cure but, rather, require expensive long-term treatment, often with an array of costly drugs. Thirdly, the increasing proportion of elderly people results is a higher incidence of cognitive impairments, such as Alzheimer's disease, and so creates an escalating demand for support services. Fourthly, although the major infectious diseases may have been eradicated in higher-income societies, their place has been taken by the 'diseases of affluence', many of them (such as diabetes and heart disease) provoked by rising levels of obesity. The resulting paradox is that, rather than making people healthier and more content with their lives, effective health care can make them less satisfied and less healthy! Moreover, this discontentment can lead to further behaviour hazardous to health, such as alcohol and drug abuse, smoking and unprotected casual sex.

DETERMINING FAIR SHARES

Since it seems inevitable that the demand for health care will always exceed the supply, it becomes necessary to think of ways in which the available resources can be fairly distributed. We can look at this on three levels: macro-, meso- and micro-allocation. The 'macro' level is concerned with how much of a country's total financial resource (its Gross Domestic Product (GDP)) is devoted to health, as compared with, say, education or defence. The 'meso' level is concerned with how the total resources available for health are distributed among different services or patient groups (for example, on acute hospitals as compared with on long-term care). The 'micro' level (sometimes called 'health care rationing') is concerned with who gets a given treatment when there is not enough to give it to everyone who is seeking it. I shall discuss all three levels, but spend most time on the third one, the rationing debate.

WHAT PRICE HEALTH?

There is a huge diversity in the percentage of GDP spent on health care across the nations of the world. The highest spender is the USA, for which the latest figure is 18 per cent. This compares with as little as 3 per cent or less spent in the poorest nations. Moreover, even though the USA is the highest spender on health care, it achieves poorer health outcomes than other countries with a lower spend. The American infant mortality rate is higher than in 30 other countries, and life expectancy is at only the 28th rank overall (OECD, 2011). Thus we can see that equitable health outcomes will not be achieved merely by spending more money on health care. There are a number of reasons for this. The first is that it is not just a matter of how much money is spent, but of how fairly it is distributed and how efficiently it is used. In countries which do not provide universal health care, like the USA, the large number of people without insurance (or with inadequate cover) avoid seeking help until a crisis strikes them, by which time they are much sicker and likely to die earlier than would have been the case if they had received care sooner. (One clear example of this is the lack of adequate prenatal care for poorer women, resulting in higher infant and maternal mortality.) A second reason is that systems which provide reimbursement to health care practitioners according to the services, treatments and tests provided give a perverse incentive both to do unnecessary tests and to over-treat with expensive drugs and procedures. (For example, there is an over-provision of magnetic resonance imaging scanners in the USA, with unnecessary usage needed to recoup the costs of investment in them. Unnecessary surgical procedures, with an associated mortality rate now much higher than that for childbirth, is another major area of concern (Gawande, 2011).) A third reason for the poor return from the high spending on health care in some countries is that health status and mortality rates are not dependent only on the provision of health care (even when it is efficient and effective). The most powerful causal factor in ill-health is poverty and its associated problems of inadequate housing, unsafe neighbourhoods, poor diet leading to malnutrition or obesity, chronic unemployment and low educational attainment. These factors are very obvious in resource-poor countries with unsafe or insufficient water, inadequate sanitation, periodic famine and violent conflicts, but in the higher-income countries the greatest health problems and shortest life expectancy also relate directly to degrees of social deprivation. Thus the price of health is not simply the amount spent (efficiently or otherwise) on health care. To achieve good outcomes in health and life expectancy, governments have to look at the whole social fabric of their country, at its welfare, housing, education and income-distribution policies as well as the efficiency and effectiveness of its health care provision and effective health education.

THE INVERSE CARE LAW

This leads us to the 'meso' level of health care allocation, since the effectiveness of health care interventions will depend not only on the total amount spent, but on the way that the total sum is distributed between different groups of people and between different types of service. I can illustrate this with a story of a village on the cliff edge. This village (so the story goes) was very picturesque, with a cosy village pub (not too constrained by licensing hours) and a wonderful view across the ocean from the cliff's edge. The only downside was that in the cold and dark winter evenings some of the villagers (after, perhaps, too jolly a time in the pub) tended to lose their way home and, straying too close to the edge of the cliff, sometimes fell over, plunging down to the rocks below and getting seriously, sometimes fatally, injured. These accidents were becoming so common that the villagers resolved to raise money for an ambulance station at the foot of the cliff with a rescue helicopter ready to get the injured rapidly to the hospital. Luckily, one of the villagers had a better (and much less costly) idea – why not erect a fence along the top of the cliff and provide better lighting in the village? (And, maybe also, why not encourage people to drink more moderately?)

This story is a parable illustrating one of the problems in health care allocation at the 'meso' level. There are very few examples of really effective health care planning that puts 'fences at the top of the cliff', as opposed to investing in the highly costly rescue services at the cliff bottom. The acute sector of medical care tends to absorb a massive proportion of the overall budget, and this is true even in low-income countries, where the obvious priority should be on community services and the provision of healthy living conditions and health education. To some extent this is quite understandable, since prevention is often much harder to achieve than crisis intervention after a potentially fatal event. Altering people's behaviour ('ensuring moderate drinking in the pub') is slow and often patchy in its effects – good examples of this problem (discussed earlier in this chapter) would be succeeding in persuading people to avoid 'junk food' or to give up smoking. It is also very hard to curb spending in the acute sector. What has been called 'shroud waving' often makes this politically impossible. When advocates for acute services warn of more deaths unless the money is spent, neither politicians nor the electorate are likely to support allocating the funds elsewhere. Yet, if we think in terms of justice as fairness, then this seems an unfair distribution of resources, since some people who could have been spared major illness or suffering will have to endure it because all the priority has been put on rescue medicine.

Another dimension of this problem relates to the commercial interests behind the promotion of health-hazardous products. Tighter control of the food industry so as to ban the unhealthy ingredients in popular and cheap food, or requiring the drinks industry to use minimum pricing so as to reduce excessive drinking would both be effective 'fences'. However, powerful lobbying by these industries makes this very difficult to achieve in some countries. Another example of the struggle between disease-prevention efforts and commercial interests is the long international saga over restrictions on cigarette packaging and advertising. It is only very recently that just one country, Australia, has managed to make it mandatory for plain packaging with accompanying graphic images of the detrimental effects of cigarette smoking to be used on all brands.

As well as dilemmas in the fair allocation of resources between types of health care intervention, there is an even more complex problem – how do we make a fair comparison between one group of patients and another, whose needs may be very different? For example, if we had a limited amount of money to spend at any given time, should it be spent on better conditions for the residential care of people suffering from dementia or on some high-cost treatment for cancer? The former might give a larger number of people a more personal and dignified form of caring, but the latter could prolong the survival of (perhaps) a smaller number of people. This kind of allocation dilemma forces us to consider how we can devise a workable theory of justice in health care, and I shall return to this below, but in the meantime we can note how hard it is to compare needs of quite different kinds. Who is to say which is the more valuable: an improved quality of what are already quite limited lives, or more months (or maybe even years) of survival with a terminal illness? We badly need some kind of sophisticated theory of justice to sort this problem out. (Watch this space!)

A third problem in allocation at the 'meso' level relates to what the British writer Tudor Hart called the 'inverse care law'. He stated it as follows: 'the availability of good medical care tends to vary inversely with the need of the population served' (Hart, 1971, p. 405). Another term for this problem is 'post code rationing' (in America it would be 'zip code'). In this case we have the unfairness of the fact that the same needs are being met unequally, because of an ethically *irrelevant* difference, namely where people live. This difference is of course true on a global scale, as we shall see later, but even in developed countries with universal health care, like the UK, there continue to be problems of inconsistency in health care provision. This problem is partly because health care practitioners prefer to work in socially desirable areas, with a patient population who are more likely to look after their own health as much as they can and who are educated and articulate. (Sometimes people in deprived areas with multiple problems are described, unkindly, as '**heartsink patients**'.) But a second problem has to do not with the availability of services but with their perceived accessibility and relevance. People can be caught in such a circle of deprivation that they tend to have lost trust in professional helpers and so avoid seeking help. Thus, the issue of access to services (in a social and psychological sense) becomes crucial. This means that any theory of justice in health care must look not only at need, but also at capacity to benefit.

DEATH BY NUMBERS – RATIONING HEALTH CARE

At the 'micro' level there is the problem of choosing who is to receive a given treatment when there are not the resources to treat everyone. A sign outside a garage is reported to have read: 'We can do good repairs, quick repairs and cheap repairs. Customers can have any two of these, but not all three.' In other words, if the repair is good and quick, it won't be cheap; if it's quick and cheap, it won't be good; and if it's good and cheap, it won't be quick! When we consider micro-allocation (usually called health care rationing) we run into a similar set of choices – good, quick or cheap? Examples of such rationing dilemmas are deciding who gets a kidney transplant when there are not enough available organs for everyone; deciding who should get priority for hip operations that will restore mobility, or cataract operations that will improve vision; providing very high-cost medication that will slow down the onset of dementia, when the budget is insufficient to treat everyone for whom it could be effective; allocating places in long-term care facilities so as to relieve the burden on families; and determining who should remain in an intensive care unit, when places are limited and fresh emergency admissions are predicted.

If we think of the notice in the garage, we recognize that, ideally, we want to give everyone treatment that is quick and good, but the problem in doing this is that we cannot afford that for everyone. So, often, at least in publicly funded provision, the cheap and good, but not quick, option is employed. In other words, a waiting list is used to ration the resource, with some people having to wait for the 'repair'. But this raises three ethical problems: dealing with the problem of queue jumping; deciding the criteria for the length of wait; and the risk of what I have called 'death by numbers', in other words, our waiting criteria may mean that some people will die before they reach the top of the queue. I shall discuss these three issues in relation to one of the problems in rationing: the allocation of kidneys for transplantation.

QUEUE JUMPING

If we think again of the notice in the garage, we see that wealthier people could take the option of 'good, quick, but not cheap', and so purchase the first-available compatible kidney (if it were legal to do this). Yet this seems unjust for at least two reasons. The first is that we do not see being wealthy as giving a person a greater right to life and health. It may be true, in fact, that richer people live longer because they can afford the kind of life style and services that promote longevity, but this does not mean that it is fair that they have this advantage. Health is not a commodity, like luxury goods available to anyone who can afford the price. Instead, health is so central to human well-being that we believe everyone (in an ideal world) should have an equal amount of it. Secondly, if ability to pay is to be the main criterion, then it seems likely that those people who could benefit more from getting the kidney will be deprived of it, since the available supply will be used up by less-sick rich people. Again this seems unfair, since ability to benefit seems to be a morally relevant difference between people, while ability to pay does not. This second objection leads us to the question of what are the right criteria for allocating places in the queue.

WHO COMES FIRST?

Imagine three people, all of whom would be medically suitable recipients of the one available kidney. The first is a young man in his early twenties. He is currently on renal dialysis, which restricts his ability to continue with some sports he enjoys and also limits his ability to get a job. He has no dependents and lives at home with his parents. The second is a married woman with two young children. She has been on dialysis longer than the first candidate and her medical condition may reduce her chances of the transplant's being an effective solution in the long term. The third is a man in his late fifties who is divorced and sees his grown up children only rarely. He has been on dialysis for several years and his chances of surviving much longer on it are poor, partly because he does not comply well with the treatment requirements, such as dietary restrictions and alcohol intake. However, a transplant is likely to give him more years of life and, without it, he will die soon. So who should get the kidney?

Some writers have suggested that we can solve dilemmas like this by a calculation of the number of years of life to be gained by the intervention multiplied by the fraction of quality of those years (where 1 is full quality and 0 is no quality). These are known as **Quality Adjusted Life Years** (QALYs). On this calculation the young man would probably get the transplant, since, as the youngest, he has the chance of survival for many years and his medical condition is such that, once off dialysis, he will probably be able to lead an active and productive life. The woman, on the other hand, has fewer years of life ahead of her and, as the transplant may be less likely to be effective, her QALY score will be further reduced. At the end of the queue is the older man, since he has fewer years again and his failures to comply may lead to problems with the transplant also. Yet, without the transplant he is almost sure to die!

WHO SHALL LIVE?

So now we have 'death by numbers', in this case the number calculated by measuring QALYs. But is this fair? This kind of calculation determines entitlement to an earlier treatment intervention in terms of ability to benefit, and so favours the young man. But both he and the woman could last longer on dialysis, whereas, if the older man is put at the end of the queue, he will certainly die quite soon. Does he deserve this, because he failed to be fully compliant with treatment in the past? Shouldn't he be given a second chance? And what about the mother with young children? Is it right that she is made to stay longer on dialysis, while the young man who has no dependents gets the most effective treatment? Maybe ability to benefit is not the only criterion we should use when deciding how to ration scarce resources.

AN INTERLUDE – TWO EXERCISES

I remarked earlier in the chapter that we will need a really sophisticated account of justice in order to deal with the problems of fair allocation that we are encountering. Now that need seems even greater, but, rather than try to spell out possible theories right away, we can approach the challenge by means of two exercises or role-play games. I shall describe two scenarios below, which require some sort of criterion for fair allocation. If you are reading this on your own, put yourself in the situation of one of the characters in the scenario and consider what solution you would offer. You can also do this in a group, or introduce it in a classroom situation, asking volunteers to take the various roles. (I have done this many times, with a very wide range of groups in the UK, New Zealand and Singapore.)

SCENARIO ONE: THE BIRTHDAY CAKE

You are at a birthday party for a six-year-old. There are five of you and you are all about the same age (either already six or soon to be). A large, round cake is brought in and someone has to decide what is a fair way to share it out. All five children like the cake and no one is allergic to it. How is the cake to be divided, and why is this fair? (Do not read on until you have decided on a solution and your reason for it.)

Several solutions may be suggested to this problem. The simplest one may be to cut the cake into equal shares, though this can be difficult with a circular shape and five pieces (unusual to have a protractor at a birthday party!). To meet this practical problem various *procedural* solutions may be suggested. One is to get a parent or other adult to cut the cake, on the assumption that they will do so impartially. Another is the 'one cuts/the others choose' procedure. This means that the person cutting will strive to make the slices equal, since the others are likely to choose any larger slices. A second type of solution is *role-related*. A parent, as the host of the party, can be seen as the one entitled to make the distribution – and well motivated to keep everyone happy! Another role-related one is to let the birthday girl or boy cut and distribute the cake. This may seem unfair at first, but, since everyone is assumed to be in this role at his or her own party, this privilege is eventually shared equally by all. A third type of solution leaves it to *individual choice*: each child can say how much they want, and these choices are unlikely to create huge disparities in sharing, since all are likely to want to be seen as fair. Finally, there is the *sharing* or *gratitude* type of solution. One of these solutions is to cut the cake into six slices (easier!), and then to offer the parent the extra slice (gratitude); another is for all to take small portions, each roughly equal, and to leave the birthday person to share the rest with their family or with friends who could not be present (sharing).

This may seem like a trivial exercise, but it does illustrate some important principles of justice. The first is the assumption of equality in justice. If no one has any special need for, or any special claim on, the cake, then either equal shares or individual choices seem fair. The cake is a luxury, not a necessity, and so no one is likely to be disadvantaged by either the attempt to cut equally or the reliance on people's sense of good behaviour in taking a share. The procedural and role-related solutions are also based on equality as a value – equally shared privilege or reliance on impartiality (symbolized by the blindfold on the figure of Justice who holds the scales in the Courts of Justice). But a new dimension comes from solutions which allow for gratitude and sharing with others, since these represent a change in orientation from 'getting' to 'giving', and suggest that even when luxury is involved, justice can be more than individual entitlement – it can also reflect communal values.

SCENARIO TWO: THE LIFEBOAT

The second scenario is a much more serious and difficult one. (The same role players should be used, but in this case there is a sixth person to consider, as we shall see.) The situation is that a lifeboat is adrift in an isolated part of the ocean with no wind. Its ship has sunk suddenly and no May-day messages have been sent. The boat has only one set of oars (no other means of propulsion) and there is no prospect of wind or rain. An inspection of the supplies shows that there is only enough food and water to last five people for four days, if shared out equally. However, it is known that the nearest land is 10 days of hard rowing away. The five characters on the boat are a frail old lady, a middle-aged sedentary worker who is somewhat overweight and has a heart condition, a young woman who is breastfeeding a baby (the sixth person) and two physically fit young men, one of whom has a mild intellectual impairment. It is also known that this second young man may have been molesting young children, though this has not been proved.

How are the rations to be shared out so that justice is ensured? (As before, think of your own answer to this problem before reading on.)

The seemingly obvious answer to this dilemma is a utilitarian one, based on the assumption that at least some of the people in the boat should be enabled to reach land and survive (the greatest happiness of the greatest number). Clearly, on this assumption, the young men are essential (and also possibly the middle-aged man). They will need enough sustenance to be able to row the boat for 10 days. The old lady is of no value in this calculation, and is unlikely to survive anyway, so should not be allowed to use up any of the precious supplies. The young woman and her baby present a problem. She will need to avoid dehydration, if she is to keep a supply of milk, so cannot row, and she will need a lot of water. It may be that, to ensure survival of at least some of the people on board, the baby will have to be allowed to die and the mother used as a fourth rower.

Of course, this is a brutal solution to the problem, and many people will shy away from it, looking for an alternative. To do this, people have to question the basic premise that survival (at least of some) must be ensured at all costs. One way of trying to avoid the logic of sacrificing some lives so as to save others is to appeal to a voluntary principle. All, it can be said, have an equal right to the rations, since everyone's life is of equal worth, but some people may choose to forego their share for the sake of the others. So, for example, the old lady may feel that she has lived a long life and that she should do all she can to help the younger people survive, even at the cost of her own life. The middle-aged man may try his best to row, though fearful that his heart could give out, and so he may die in the attempt. It will be hardest for the young mother. How can she offer to abandon her baby and help the others survive? It seems unlikely that she would do so, without being coerced into it. Thus, little help may come from the voluntary principle. The baby may have to be forcefully sacrificed.

A different solution entirely is to reject totally the assumption that survival (at least of some) is all that matters. Survival with dishonour and an enduring sense of guilt could be worse than death. Therefore, the value of each person's life is ranked equally and the group must co-operate to give everyone enough food and water, even at the cost of never reaching land. In this account, justice means responding proportionately to each person's need, without discrimination against anyone on grounds of utility.

PRINCIPLES FOR JUST HEALTH CARE

We can now return to the problem of finding an adequate theory of justice in situations of scarcity of health care. Based on the above scenarios, we can see several possible principles that might be used to decide how to allocate fairly:

1   To each an equal share
2   To each according to individual choice
3   To each according to potential for future life years
4   To each according to what they deserve
5   To each according to their social usefulness
6   To each according to their needs.

We have seen already that in situations of necessity (health or survival on the lifeboat), as opposed to situations of luxury (the birthday cake), equal shares do not seem to be fair, since this will mean some people will have more than they need and some less. The second principle also causes problems, since we cannot guarantee that people will make individual choices that are fair to everyone. (However, there may be another way of enabling individual choice, through an agreement on fair procedures, and I shall return to this later.) The third option, life-years ahead, seems acceptable as an individual choice (the old lady volunteers to starve), but if this is imposed on people it leads to unacceptable ageist discrimination. Groups doing the exercise rarely go for the fourth option (desert or merit), though some may think of it in relation to the suspected child abuser. (In the birthday party the person who has the birthday can be seen as deserving special treatment, but then each person will have the same special day.) The main problem with the notion of desert is that it can be both subjective and inconsistent. For example, we may say that persistent smokers deserve lung cancer, since they could have prevented it, but then how far will this principle extend? Do obese people deserve their diabetes, highly stressed executives their heart attacks? We do not know how far we can hold people individually responsible for their detrimental conditions – and this is certainly true of the ambiguous situation of the young man with intellectual disability. Thus, a desert or merit principle can be seen as posing the danger of being unfair.

This leaves us with two principles: one based on utility and the other on needs or rights. These correspond to two of the ethical theories we discussed in Chapter 2, utilitarian theory and deontological theory. In the former theory, social benefit is the final arbiter. Ideally all individuals should have the hope of happiness or well-being, but, since (as Jeremy Bentham said) 'all shall count as one and none as more than one', the individual will have to be subordinated to the welfare of the majority. When this is applied to health care rationing, some groups would have to be favoured over others, since they have more to contribute to the general welfare, and so the allocation of resources to those who are of little or no use to society would be unjust to the majority. This theory, if followed to its logical conclusion, would have serious consequences for health care provision. For example, it implies that the state should not pay for facilities for the severely intellectually disabled (though parents could be allowed to pay for them out of their own resources), and it would seem to give priority to young, highly qualified persons who can contribute best to the prosperity of the society, at the expense of the elderly and those who are physically or mentally chronically ill. These logical outcomes of utilitarian theory have led people to see it as 'brutal' or 'inhumane', like the scenario on the lifeboat that sacrifices both the baby and the old woman. On the other hand, as we shall see, those theories that argue for an equal consideration of everyone's needs can be seen as impossible to implement. Thus, some people may favour some form of moderated utility theory, where some attention would be paid to the needs of the non-productive members of society (in consideration of the unhappiness the majority would feel if they were totally neglected), but priority would clearly be given to those who can create most social benefit.

The alternative, deontologically based theory sees every human being as equally deserving of consideration and respect, and so everyone should have equal access to services that meet their health needs. But how will this work in practice, when there are simply not enough resources to meet everyone's needs? The UN Declaration of Human Rights (1948) states:

> Everyone has the right to a standard of living adequate for the health and well-being of himself and his family, including food, clothing, housing and medical care and necessary social services, and the right to security in the event of unemployment, sickness, disability, widowhood, old age or other lack of livelihood in circumstances beyond his control.
>
> (United Nations, 1948, Article 25 (1))

We should notice that this is not the 'complete physical, mental and social well-being' advocated by the WHO Charter. It is describing a threshold, a basic minimum, below which no one should be allowed to fall. How, then, might this minimum be defined? Answering this question requires us to look first at general theories of distributional justice, other than the utilitarian one just discussed, and see how this might help us to define a basic minimum health status.

The most influential of such theories has been that of the political philosopher John Rawls. In his monumental work, *A Theory of Justice* (1973), Rawls imagines a hypothetical situation in which people who are free and rational but under a 'veil of ignorance' would decide what kind of society they would wish to be members of. The 'veil of ignorance' ensures that they know nothing about their own abilities, likes and dislikes, conception of the good, or position in society. Rawls argues that the rational way of ensuring that this society is fair to everyone would be to agree to two fundamental principles of justice. He calls these the **Liberty Principle** and the **Difference Principle**. These principles are in 'lexical order', which means that if there is conflict between the principles, then the first one must take priority. This approach to justice can be called a 'social contract' theory, since it is based on the idea that, given a choice, people would agree to this kind of social arrangement. (We can see that this is one way of using the voluntary approach to gain agreement to a fair procedure, but it is very theoretical, since no one *actually* makes an agreement of this kind.)

Rawls (1973) defines the fundamental principles of justice as follows:

First principle
  Each person is to have an equal right to the most extensive total system of equal basic liberties compatible with a similar system of liberty for all.
Second principle
  Social and economic inequalities are to be arranged so that they are both: (1) to the greatest benefit of the least advantaged ... and (2) attached to offices and positions open to all under conditions of fair equality of opportunity.

(p. 302)

We can see at once that Rawls does not believe that justice requires that everyone have an *equal share* of social or economic resources. He argues that differences in income and social status are inevitable in a free society (and also perhaps desirable, since they will motivate people to achieve improvements in their status). Justice requires only that people have an *equal opportunity* to improve their situation, but he does concede that attention should be paid to improving the lot of those most disadvantaged by the social and economic differences. This is known as the 'maximin' principle, and it would (Rawls believes) prevent massive exploitation of the poorest members of society merely in order to make the rich richer.

So where does health status come into this theory? Another philosopher, Norman Daniels, has proposed that we can include this in the requirements for equal opportunity. He claims that, since ill-health can severely compromise a person's ability to pursue their life plans, justice requires that we remove the disadvantages caused by health and disability. This means that people have a right to those health care interventions that will allow them to pursue the 'normal opportunity range' for their society (allowing for differences here according to a person's age or degree of disability). So a person will be below the threshold for a minimum health status when they are not enabled to make the range of choices that others with an acceptable level of health (but like them in all other relevant respects) are able to make (Daniels, 2008).

Another writer, Lennart Nordenfeldt, has offered a similar criterion, since he also refers to a person's capacity to pursue his or her chosen goals in life. Nordenfeldt (1987) refers to these as 'vital goals' and he defines health as follows:

> A is in health if, and only if, A has the ability, given standard circumstances, to realize his vital goals, i.e. the set of goals which are necessary and together sufficient for his minimal happiness.
>
> (p. 97)

A feature of both of these accounts of health is that they do not refer to the absence of disease as the main criterion. In fact, both accounts would allow for us to describe a sick, or even dying person, as healthy if he or she could pursue those goals, which are seen as 'vital' to them (Nordenfeldt), or which it would be reasonable for anyone else in these circumstances to be able to pursue (Daniels). So, for example, we might say that a minimal threshold of health care provision for dying patients is that they be provided with adequate terminal care, so that they can be sufficiently free from pain, indignity and distress to say goodbye to those they love. They ought to be enabled to pursue their 'life plan' for their dying days.

Such accounts of the nature of health are relatively modest in their criteria for a decent minimum of health care, and so may be of some help in the dilemma about rationing scarce resources. For example, they may help to moderate the tendency to use highly expensive interventions to keep people alive at all costs, even when they are left in a state in which they have no opportunity to pursue any life goals any more, or even to communicate with those they love. But they do leave some unanswered problems. One is the allocation of life-changing interventions (such as organ transplants) when all potential recipients could benefit in terms of approaching more closely to the 'normal opportunity range' or having a better chance of realizing their 'vital goals'. And there is a more profound problem: because these accounts make the definition of health relative to a person's specific society, or to personal awareness of what will make them happy (a totally subjective definition of health), they are in danger of overlooking gross disparities in health status both within nations and between nations. If a person has learned to live with a very low expectation of what is needed to make them happy, or if people live in societies or groups where the overall health status is very low, are we to say that they have been treated justly? Is there no more objective criterion of what is simply not humanely acceptable as a 'normal range' of health? That question raises the issue of global inequity in health, to which I now turn.

GLOBAL INEQUITY IN HEALTH

The statistics on health inequalities in the world as a whole paint a grim picture. A child born in Swaziland is nearly 30 times more likely to die before the age of five than a child born in Sweden. (There are 119 deaths per thousand births in Swaziland, compared with 4 in Sweden.) A child in Cambodia is 17 times more likely to die in its first five years than is a child in Canada. Worldwide, one death in three is from communicable disease (examples include AIDS/HIV, tuberculosis, polio, malaria and measles), yet almost all these deaths occur in the low-income countries. The relative infrequency of death due to communicable disease in the industrialized world shows what could be achieved if there were a real commitment to global health equality (UC Atlas of Global Inequality).

In 2008 the WHO published the final report of its Commission on Social Determinants of Health. The report pointed out that:

> Where systematic differences in health are judged to be avoidable by reasonable action they are, quite simply, unfair ... Putting right these inequities – the huge and remediable differences in health between and

within countries – is a matter of social justice ... Social injustice is killing people on a grand scale.

(World Health Organization, 2008, p. 3)

The Commission argued that lack of access to health care is only one small part of the array of social determinants that create this injustice. The other factors are 'caused by the unequal distribution of power, income, goods, and services, globally and nationally (p. 4)'. As a result of this people not only lack adequate health care, they also have inadequate and insanitary living conditions, minimal or no education, dangerous work environments and insufficient income to support themselves and their families. The report urges action in three areas in all the countries with poor health outcomes (including richer countries with disadvantaged groups):

1   Improve daily living conditions;
2   Tackle the inequitable distribution of power, money and resources;
3   Measure and understand the problem, and assess the impact of possible actions to deal with it.

The importance of this approach to global health inequity is that it broadens the debate from the worries of the richer countries about escalating health care costs to more fundamental questions about the basic social arrangements in a society. Of course, this is a politically difficult move to make, and the WHO does not have the power to make governments and international commercial and financial institutions change the policies that are causing such massive health problems for the majority of the world's population. In terms of bioethical theory, however, this broader canvas for looking at justice in health seems essential. It is no longer possible to contain the discussion of health priorities within national boundaries, and to recognize this we have to make the move from a 'right to health care' to a 'right to health'. I shall now discuss an alternative theory of health justice which attempts to do this.

THE CAPABILITY TO BE HEALTHY (CH) THEORY

The theories we have looked at so far either are based on majority benefit (utilitarianism) or on some kind of social contract based on a specific society's norms (the 'normal opportunity range' of Daniels or the 'vital goals' account of Nordenfeldt). But an alternative approach to both of these theories is one which sees a universal right to health, based on an understanding of the equal worth and dignity of every human being. This is a theory of moral entitlement, based on the accounts of two contemporary philosophers, Amartya Sen (2009) and Martha Nussbaum, but fully developed in Sridhar Ventatapuram's book *Health Justice* (2011). The theory asks the question: What is every human being morally entitled to in terms of their health status? To answer this, it considers the four factors that are the causes of an individual's health and longevity. These are: biological endowments and needs, individual behaviours, physical environment and social conditions. Injustice in relation to health occurs when people suffer premature death or impairments, *which are preventable*. The CH theory argues that while the biological endowment probably cannot be significantly changed and the health-destructive or -enhancing behaviours of an individual are that person's responsibility, the health-destructive effects of both the physical and social environments (the factors identified above by the WHO report) *are* able to be changed. Thus, there is a social obligation, not to achieve perfect health outcomes (since these will also depend on biological and personal responsibility factors), but to alter those physical and social conditions which destroy health, and to change them into ones which enhance people's *capacity to be healthy*. Health injustice occurs when, nationally and internationally, we fail to make those changes that would give people a real chance to lead longer and healthier lives. Although this theory is not in any sense a religious one, its basic premise is perhaps summed up in the 'Serenity Prayer' of Alcoholics Anonymous (a prayer originally written by the American theologian Reinhold Niebuhr):

> God, grant me the serenity to accept the things I cannot change,
> The courage to change the things I can,
> And the wisdom to know the difference.

Of course, this prayer relates to individual serenity and resolve, but its message about the courage to change echoes the challenge of this approach. Like the WHO document, it is arguing that failure to tackle those social factors that reduce people's capability for health is 'killing people on a grand scale', and so cannot be seen as morally right.

However, this theory is still at a somewhat general level. What are the specific capabilities that are needed to enhance health and to ensure that there is a universal respect for human dignity? Martha Nussbaum (2006) suggests a list of attainable human capabilities that we should see as normative. They are:

1   Being able to live a normal length of lifespan;
2   Having good health;
3   Maintain bodily integrity;
4   Being able to use senses, imagination and think;
5   Having emotions and emotional attachments;
6   Possess practical reason to form a conception of the good;
7   Have social affiliations that are meaningful and respectful;
8   Express concern for other species;
9   Be able to play;
10   Have control over one's material and political environment.

(Nussbaum, 2006, p. 76–77)

We can see that, with such a wide-ranging list, we are getting back to the holistic definition of health in the WHO charter. The list does not help us to make rationing decisions because of the lack of specification in its terms. For example, what is 'good health'? And how do we define a 'normal lifespan', when life expectancy, at least in the richer countries, is constantly rising? Some other items in the list may not be attainable by everyone, for example, by those with severe physical impairments. But, like the WHO definition, it can set a horizon for health improvement, reminding us that human life has a whole set of dimensions to it, all of which are components of what we should see as health in the broadest sense. Thus, this third kind of justice theory, the 'capability approach', takes us back to VE, where human fulfilment is the ultimate goal. We still may not know to whom to give the kidney. However, we can more easily see how social and political policies threaten human dignity on a global scale. Returning to the earlier exercise, we can realize that there is no adequate answer to the moral dilemma of those on board the lifeboat, but at least we can see that there have to be better lifeboats! Thus, eventually bioethics theory can lead to demands for socio-political change.

BIRDS ON THE WING

Another story may help to clarify the kind of moral approach that the CH theory aspires to. Some years ago I was a speaker at a conference in New Zealand looking at the controversy over cannabis use and health. I was going to use an image of bird flight from the writings of Immanuel Kant. He described the folly of a dove resenting the resistance of the air against its wings, imagining that without this it could fly much faster – but of course, without air resistance the dove could not fly at all! So, said Kant, we need the resistance of facts to make our theories work, for without facts our ideas are useless. I was going to say a similar thing about avoiding a debate about cannabis uninformed by reliable data. But I dropped this idea when, in the speech before mine, a Maori health activist used a quite different image of flight to point out how our society failed to care for those prone to drug abuse. Here is how I described his speech when I wrote about it later in my book *Health as Liberation* (1995):

> He spoke of the migration of flocks of birds and of how, as we see them in their graceful and near miraculous flight, we only half perceive what is going on. He spoke of how the lead birds take turns in meeting the resistance of the air and how the aerodynamic shape they create makes possible the long flight of the whole flock. He spoke of how the young and the old and the frail are sheltered within the wedge shape and of how, if a bird is injured or too tired to continue, stronger birds will accompany it down to a resting place and then help it to rejoin the flock still circling overhead.

(p. 3)

Of course, this is instinctive behaviour by the birds, not some kind of moral choice, and human beings are not birds! But the image suggests that we might hope for a human world where such care, protection and encouragement to venture on become the norm for international co-operation in health.

GLOBAL SURVIVAL

Still, even if this were to happen at least in part (and health inequities have already been reduced over the past decade), it may all be too late. An even greater threat faces our generation: the global survival of the human species itself. This is where bioethics overlaps with environmental ethics, since there is now a constant stream of evidence that human life on earth will be unsustainable if we continue to use resources as we do at present. There are two major and interrelated aspects to this threat to human survival: global warming and population expansion. So far as the former is concerned, the WHO report (2008) discussed in the previous section pointed to the risk posed by the increasing urbanization of the world's population:

> The current model of urbanization poses significant environmental challenges, particularly climate change – the impact of which is greater in low-income countries and among vulnerable subpopulations. At present, greenhouse gas emissions are determined mainly by consumption patterns in cities of the developed world. Transport and buildings contribute 21 per cent to CO_2 emissions, agricultural activity accounts for about one fifth. And yet crop yields depend in large part on prevailing climate conditions. The disruption and depletion of the climate system and the task of reducing global health inequities go hand in hand.
>
> (p. 10)

Thus, the failure to control greenhouse gas emissions in the major industrialized countries has a direct effect on the health and, eventually, the survival of those in the poorest parts of the world. But the second factor will eventually affect the whole of the world population: this is the depletion of the world's resources overall by current population trends and patterns of consumption. This has been fully documented in a report by the Royal Society of London, *People and the Planet* (2012). The report points out that 'on a finite planet there are environmental constraints on human population growth and material and energy consumption. Some limits may already have been reached, and fundamental human needs for food, energy and water are at risk' (Royal Society of

London, 2012, p. 82). So we can see that the most significant of all bioethical issues that we have to confront at the present time is not concerned with the dilemmas of health care or with the confusing range of choices that new medical technologies raise from birth to death. Greater than all these challenges is whether we can safeguard our planet and the life upon it for ourselves and future generations. The Royal Society's report makes it clear that this can happen only if governments throughout the world take decisive action now. It makes a series of recommendations, of which the following are the most urgent (see pp. 99 and 101 of the report):

- The most immediate way to reduce the negative impact of human activity on the planet is to reduce material consumption of those who currently consume the most.
- It is of the utmost urgency to reduce consumption and emissions that are already causing damage, for example greenhouse gases, deforestation, and land use change amongst others.
- Furthermore, unless the goal is a world in which extreme inequality persists, it is necessary to make space for those in poverty, especially the 1.3 billion people living in absolute poverty, to achieve an adequate standard of living.
- Longer-term, the stabilization of the population is essential to avoid further exceeding planetary limits and increasing poverty. This will mean more effective (but not compulsory) use of contraception in countries with high fertility rates.

(Royal Society of London, 2012, p. 99–101)

This final bioethical issue is not really one for debate or uncertainty, for who could doubt that such global survival is absolutely imperative? Of course, there is debate about the extent of the crisis, even in some cases about the accuracy of predictions about global warming (though this is a view often funded by enterprises with a financial stake in denying it). People will also differ in how best to deal with the ecological crisis, and decisive political action is proving very hard to achieve worldwide. However, the scientific credentials of the Royal Society of London (2012) are beyond doubt, and we need to heed its final warning:

Over the next 30–40 years the confluence of the challenges described in this report provides the opportunity to move towards a sustainable economy and a better world for the majority of humanity, or alternatively the risk of social, economic and environmental failures and catastrophes on a scale never imagined.

(p. 105)

FURTHER READING

The various reports mentioned in this chapter can make sobering reading, but are probably essential for us all if we are to make any significant change to the present situation globally, before it is all too late. For the debates about public health you can refer to the following website: http://phsj.org/ and also to the journal *Public Health Ethics*. The health-rationing debate is well aired in the various readers in bioethics mentioned in the earlier chapters, but if you want to think more about how the market can jeopardize justice, I can recommend Michael Sandel's latest book, *What Money Can't Buy: The Moral Limits of Markets* (2012). See also www.justice. harvard.org. On global injustice in health, the following website gives up-to-date figures: http://sasi.group.shef.ac.uk/. If you want to think more deeply about how justice relates to development, the best source will be Amartya Sen's *Development as Freedom* (1999). Justice theory is not an easy part of bioethics to make sense of, since the issues are very complex ones. While we often know injustice when we see it, we can find it very hard to describe clearly. The various writings of Rawls, Nussbaum and Sen referred to in the references for this chapter are not for the faint-hearted, but trying to understand them at least in part could be well worth the effort. Finally, when considering if our planet has a future, you might want to read *Silent Spring* by Rachel Carson (1963), a classic in the field. There are also two journals dealing with the ethical issues, *Environmental Ethics* and *Environmental Values*.

APPENDIX

THE HIPPOCRATIC OATH

I swear by Apollo the Physician and Asclepius and Hygeia and Panaceia and all the gods and goddesses, making them my witnesses, that I will fulfil according to my ability and judgment this oath and this covenant:

To hold him who has taught me this art as equal to my parent and to live my life in partnership with him, and if he is in need of money to give him a share of mine, and to regard his offspring as equal to my brothers in male lineage and to teach them this art – if they desire to learn it – without fee and covenant; to give share of precepts and oral instruction and all other learning to my sons and to the sons of him who has instructed me and to pupils who have signed the covenant and have taken an oath according to the medical law, but to no one else.

I will apply dietetic measure for the benefit of the sick according to my ability and judgment; I will keep them from harm and injustice. I will neither give a deadly drug to anybody if asked for it, nor will I make a suggestion to this effect. Similarly I will not give a woman an abortive remedy. In purity and in holiness I will guard my life and my art.

I will not use the knife, not even on sufferers from stone, but will withdraw in favour of such men as are engaged in this work.

Whatever houses I may visit, I will come for the benefit of the sick, remaining free of all intentional injustice, of all mischief and in particular of sexual relations with both female and male persons, be they free or slaves.

What I may see or hear in the course of the treatment or even outside of the treatment in regard to the life of men, which on no account one must spread abroad, I will keep to myself holding such things shameful to be spoken about.

If I fulfil this oath and do not violate it, may it be granted to me to enjoy life and art, being honoured with fame among all men for all time to come; if I transgress it and swear falsely, may the opposite be my lot.

THE WORLD MEDICAL ASSOCIATION DECLARATION OF GENEVA

Adopted by the 2nd General Assembly of the World Medical Association, Geneva, Switzerland, September 1948 and amended by the 22nd World Medical Assembly, Sydney, Australia, August 1968 and the 35th World Medical Assembly, Venice, Italy, October 1983 and the 46th WMA General Assembly, Stockholm, Sweden, September 1994 and editorially revised by the 170th WMA Council Session, Divonne-les-Bains, France, May 2005 and the 173rd WMA Council Session, Divonne-les-Bains, France, May 2006

AT THE TIME OF BEING ADMITTED AS A MEMBER OF THE MEDICAL PROFESSION:

- I SOLEMNLY PLEDGE to consecrate my life to the service of humanity;
- I WILL GIVE to my teachers the respect and gratitude that is their due;
- I WILL PRACTISE my profession with conscience and dignity;
- THE HEALTH OF MY PATIENT will be my first consideration;

- I WILL RESPECT the secrets that are confided in me, even after the patient has died;
- I WILL MAINTAIN by all the means in my power, the honour and the noble traditions of the medical profession;
- MY COLLEAGUES will be my sisters and brothers;
- I WILL NOT PERMIT considerations of age, disease or disability, creed, ethnic origin, gender, nationality, political affiliation, race, sexual orientation, social standing or any other factor to intervene between my duty and my patient;
- I WILL MAINTAIN the utmost respect for human life;
- I WILL NOT USE my medical knowledge to violate human rights and civil liberties, even under threat;
- I MAKE THESE PROMISES solemnly, freely and upon my honour.

EXTRACT FROM CHARAKA SAMHITA'S OATH OF INITIATION:

Day and night, however thou mayest be engaged, thou shalt endeavor for the relief of patients with all thy heart and soul.

Thou shalt not desert or injure thy patient for the sake of thy life or thy living. Thou shalt not commit adultery even in thought.

Even so, thou shalt not covet other's possessions.

WORLD MEDICAL ASSOCIATION DECLARATION OF HELSINKI – ETHICAL PRINCIPLES FOR MEDICAL RESEARCH INVOLVING HUMAN SUBJECTS

Please refer to http://www.wma.net/en/30publications/10policies/b3/.

GLOSSARY

Anorexia The term literally means 'lack of appetite', but it is often used as the short description of the medical condition Anorexia Nervosa, which is an eating disorder characterized by immoderate food restriction and irrational fear of gaining weight, as well as a distorted body self-perception.

Autonomy/Autonomous Literally the term means 'self-rule', from the Greek words *autos* (self) and *nomos* (law). In ethics the term is used to describe behaviour or choices which are consistent with a person's long-term goals. So an autonomous individual will make decisions based on their own values, rather than simply following the commands of others.

Biobanks Large collections of human tissue (such as blood samples) with associated links to extensive health records relating to the donors of the samples. These large collections can be used to carry out extensive research into the causes and potential cures of diseases of all kinds, often with the use of genetic analyses.

Bio-commons A term used to claim that human tissue should not be regarded as merely the personal property of those maintaining collections of such material but, rather, as a resource available to everyone who seeks to carry out research on such samples for human benefit. The term derives from the historical concept of common grazing land, which was to be available to the whole community, rather than to those claiming it as personal property.

Brain death   Brain death is defined as irreversible unconsciousness with complete loss of brain function, including the brain stem, although the heartbeat may continue.

Bulimia   An eating disorder in which the affected person feels compelled to eat large quantities of food and then to purge himself or herself of the food by using laxatives or through vomiting. Those affected frequently also suffer from **Anorexia** (see above).

Cadaver   A preserved dead human body used for anatomical dissection.

Categorical imperative   A moral command that must be obeyed absolutely and without exceptions. According to Immanuel Kant, all genuine moral requirements must be in this form, and if they are not then they are merely hypothetical or conditional (see **Hypothetical** imperative).

Cloning   The production of an identical, or nearly identical, copy of an individual. Distinction is sometimes made between 'reproductive cloning', which produces an offspring identical with the individual from whom the cells have been taken, and 'therapeutic cloning', in which identical cells are produced but are not used to create another individual. The production of Dolly the sheep is an example of reproductive cloning. Cloned cells for therapeutic purposes might be used to help repair damaged cells in the same individual, or even to produce genetically compatible organs for transplantation.

Cognitive impairments   The inability to reason or to understand reason or to understand, which could be expected of a person of normal intelligence. This may be caused by intellectual disabilities from birth, or may be the result of brain injury later in life or of the onset of senile dementia. The term is a contentious one, since the definition of what is 'normal' can be regarded as socially determined and potentially resulting in prejudice against large groups of people.

Communitarianism   A type of moral theory which stresses the primary importance of community benefit or social values, requiring the individual members of society to make their personal desires subservient to the common good.

Conjoined twins   An extremely rare type of identical twins who are physically joined at birth. Some conjoined twins are attached at the upper body, others may be joined at the waist and share a pair of legs. Conjoined twins often share major organs such as a heart, liver or brain.

Consequentialism   A group of moral theories which argue that morally right decisions and policies can be ascertained by estimating the overall balance of good and bad consequences of any given action or social policy. (See **Utilitarianism**.)

Cyclothymic mood disorder   A form of severe mental illness in which the person alternates between periods of high elation, or 'mania', and periods of deep depression. Previously known as 'manic depressive psychosis'.

Deontology/Deontological theory   Deontology is a type of ethical theory that bases moral requirements on the concept of duty (from the Greek, *deon*, meaning 'it is required'). There are various forms of deontological theory, of which the best known is that of the German philosopher Immanuel Kant.

Difference Principle   One of the basic principles of the theory of justice formulated by the legal philosopher John Rawls. The principle allows for differences in wealth and other social advantages in a society, but only in so far as such differences can be shown to bring greater benefit to the least-well off than can any other social arrangement.

Embryonic stem cells   Embryonic stem cells, as their name suggests, are derived from embryos. Most ESCs are derived from embryos that develop from eggs that have been fertilized *in vitro* and then donated for research purposes. Embryonic stem cells are distinguished by two properties: their pluripotency and their ability to replicate indefinitely. Pluripotency distinguishes ESCs from adult stem cells; while ESCs can generate all cell types in the body, adult stem cells are multipotent and can produce only a limited number of cell types.

Evidence-based medicine   A theoretical approach to medicine that requires that, as far as possible, decisions about treatment should be based on the best available evidence, derived from well-designed trials of the various options.

Germline modification   A form of manipulation of human or animal genes which affects not just the individual whose genes are being modified but also any descendants of that individual, since the altered genes will be passed down the generations through reproduction.

Heartsink patients A pejorative term sometimes used to describe patients who have a complex set of problems, some of them medical and others more related to social causes, but who frequently seek medical attention, even though this is unlikely to be effective in helping them.

High-impact journals Academic journals which have a high circulation in the scientific community and whose articles are frequently cited by other authors.

Human enhancement An approach to the physical or mental capacities of individuals which aims not simply to overcome any current defects or disabilities through therapeutic measures but to make temporary or permanent improvements in some physical or mental capacities. For example, improvements in attention span or memory may be attempted in an educational context; or enhanced physical abilities such as speed and stamina, in a sporting context.

Human genome The human genome is stored on 23 chromosome pairs in the cell nucleus and in DNA. The Human Genome Project produced a reference sequence of the human genome which is used worldwide in the biomedical sciences.

Hypothetical imperative A rule or command which need be obeyed only if we wish to achieve the outcome it promises. For example, 'If you want to remain healthy, take regular exercise'. The philosopher Immanuel Kant argued that such imperatives could not be the basis of morality, since acting morally was an absolute requirement on all rational human beings and so could not be subject to individual choice or desires (see **Categorical imperative** above).

Induced pluripotent stem cells Induced pluripotent stem cells (iPSCs) are adult cells that have been genetically reprogrammed to an ESC-like state by being forced to express genes and factors important for maintaining the defining properties of ESCs.

Libertarianism An approach to ethics which stresses the importance of the freedom of each individual to make his or her own moral choices, thus opposing, or minimizing, the intrusion of the society on individual choice. This approach is in sharp contrast with **Communitarianism** (see above).

Liberty Principle   The first and most important principle in John Rawls' theory of justice, which requires that all persons have an equal right to a set of basic human liberties.

Medical tourism   Also called medical travel or health tourism. A term initially coined by travel agencies and the mass media to describe the practice of travelling across international borders to obtain health care.

Morbidity   An illness or an abnormal condition or quality; (in health statistics) the rate at which an illness or abnormality occurs, calculated by dividing the number of people who are affected within a group by the entire number of people in that group; the rate at which an illness occurs in a particular area or population.

Obsessive compulsive disorder   A psychiatric illness in which the person feels compelled to carry out certain actions (for example, constant hand washing) or always to do things in a set order (for example, an order for actions for getting ready for bed). Frequently, affected individuals will fear that they have forgotten something or not done it correctly and so will repeat the action over and over again.

Pandemics   A pandemic (from Greek *pan* 'all' and *demos* 'people') is an epidemic of infectious disease that has spread through human populations across a large region; for instance, across multiple continents, or even worldwide.

Paranoid delusions   A symptom of severe mental illness (psychosis) in which the person is convinced that they are being persecuted or stalked by people meaning to do them harm. Such delusions can sometimes lead the person to carry out violent acts in what they believe to be self-defence.

Pharmacological constraints   Drugs used to control the behaviour of individuals, without the need of physical constraints. These may range from drugs to control severe psychiatric symptoms to sleeping pills and tranquillizers used to control the wandering of patients with dementia.

Phobias   Irrational fears, for example of open spaces ('agoraphobia') or of being shut in a closed space ('claustraphobia').

Prognosis   The prediction of the likely course and outcome of a medical condition and of the likely effects of any therapeutic interventions.

Quality Adjusted Life Years (QALYs)   A method of measuring the effectiveness of treatments by estimating the gain in quality of life achieved by the intervention and then multiplying that by the number of extra years of life that the treatment is thought to achieve.

Regenerative medicine   The use of stem cells to repair defects in the body, for example, by repairing spinal damage or correcting neural disorders such as Parkinson's Disease.

Schizophrenia   A group of severe brain disorders in which people interpret reality abnormally. It may result in some combination of hallucinations, delusions and disordered thinking and behaviour.

Somatic Cell Nuclear Transfer   The technique whereby the nucleus of a cell from part of one body is transferred to a cell from another body, from which the nucleus has been removed. This results in the reprogrammed cell splitting and reproducing itself in a form almost identical to that of the cell from which the nucleus was taken. This technique enables **cloning** (see above).

Surrogacy   An arrangement whereby a woman agrees to become pregnant for the purpose of gestating and giving birth to a child for others to raise. The surrogate mother may be partly genetically related to the child (if her egg is fertilized to create the pregnancy), or not at all genetically related, when an embryo created from the egg and sperm of others (possiby the commissioning couple) is implanted in her uterus.

Therapeutic misconception   The mistaken belief that if one takes part in a clinical trial of a drug or other therapy it will always bring a treatment benefit. Since most trials work on a system whereby patients are randomized to either a control group or an experimental group, the belief is mistaken, since any one person may receive an inactive substance or the less-effective of two remedies being compared.

Utilitarianism   A type of consequentialist theory (see **Consequentialism**) formulated by the philosopher Jeremy Bentham and refined by his follower John Stuart Mill, in which good is calculated by estimating the greatest amount of happiness and the least amount of pain for the greatest number of people (the Greatest Happiness Principle).

Virtue ethics An approach to ethics first formulated by the ancient Greek philosophers in which the character of the moral agent is the most important determinant of moral actions.

REFERENCES

Andrews, L. and Nelkin, D. (2001). *Body Bazaar: The Market for Human Tissue in the Biotechnology Age*, New York: Crown.

Ashcroft, R. E., Dawson, A., Draper, H. et al. (eds) (2007). *Principles of Health Care Ethics*, London: John Wiley & Sons.

BBC. (2009a). Abortion: The Church of England and Roman Catholic Church views on abortion. *Religions* [Online]. Available at: http://www.bbc.co.uk/religion/religions/christianity/christianethics/abortion_1.shtml [Accessed 17 August 2012].

—— (2009c). Hackers target leading climate research unit. *BBC* [Online]. Available at: http://news.bbc.co.uk/2/hi/science/nature/8370282.stm [Accessed 12 September 2012].

Beauchamp, T. L. and Childress, J. F. (2012). *Principles of Biomedical Ethics*, 7th edn, New York: Oxford University Press.

Beecher, H. K. (1970). *Research and the Individual*, Boston: Little, Brown.

Bentham, J. (1879). *Introduction to the Principles of Morals and Legislation*, Oxford: The Clarendon Press.

Berlin, I. (1958). *Four Essays on Liberty*, Oxford: Clarendon Press.

Biller-Andorno, N. (2002). Gender imbalance in living organ donation. *Medicine, Health Care and Philosophy*, 5, 199–204.

Black, E. (2003). *War against the Weak: Eugenics and America's Campaign to Create a Master Race*, New York: Four Walls Eight Windows.

Bok, S. (1978). *Lying: Moral Choice in Public and Private Life*, New York: Pantheon Books.

British Medical Association. (1974). *Medical Ethics*, London: British Medical Association House.

Brody, J. E. (1974). Charge of false research data stirs cancer scientists at Sloan-Kettering. *New York Times*.

Campbell, A. V. (1995). *Health as Liberation: Medicine, Theology and the Quest for Justice*, Cleveland, OH: The Pilgrim Press.

—— (1998). The 'ethics of care' as virtue ethics. In: Evans, M. (ed.) *Critical Reflection on Medical Ethics*, Standford, CT: Jai Press.

—— (2009). *The Body in Bioethics*, London: Routledge.

Campbell, A. V., Gillett, G. and Jones, G. (2006). *Medical Ethics*, Oxford: Oxford University Press.

Capps, B. and Campbell, A. V. (eds) (2010). *Contested Cells: Global Perspectives on the Stem Cell Debate*, London: Imperial College Press.

Carson, R. (1963). *Silent Spring*, Louise: Houghton Mifflin Harcourt.

Cathcart, T. and Klein, D. L. (2008). *Plato and a Platypus Walk into a Bar ... Understanding Philosophy through Jokes*, New York: Penguin Books.

CBS News Staff. (2012). Abortion more common where it's illegal: where are rates highest? *CBS News*, 19 January 2012.

Chong, K.-C. (1999). The practice of Jen. *Philosophy East and West*, 49, 298–316.

Cicirelli, V. (2001). Personal meanings of death in older adults and young adults in relation to their fears of death. *Death Studies*, 25, 663–83.

Consultative Expert Working Group on Research and Development: Financing and Coordination. (2012). Report of the Consultative Expert Working Group on Research and Development: Financing and Coordination. World Health Organization.

Cua, A. S. (2002). The ethical and the religious dimensions of Li (rites). *Review of Metaphysics*, 55, 471–519.

Daniels, N. (2008). *Just Health Care: Meeting Health Needs Fairly*, Cambridge: Cambridge University Press.

Department of Labor, Department of Health and Human Services, Equal Employment Opportunity Commission et al. *Genetic Information and the Workplace* [Online]. Available at: http://www.genome.gov/10001732 [Accessed 29 October 2011].

Dhand, A. (2002). 'The *Dharma* of ethics and ethics of *Dharma*.' *Journal of Religious Ethics*, 30, 347–72.

Donne, J. (2002). from For whom this bell tolls (Meditation XVII). In: Roberts, T. and Al, E. (eds) *The Broadview Anthology of Expository Prose*, Peterborough, Ont.: Broadview Press.

Elliott, C. and Kramer, P. D. (2004). *Better than Well: American Medicine Meets the American Dream*, New York: W. W. Norton.

Emanuel, E. K., Crouch, R. A., Arras, J. D. et al. (2003). *Ethical and Regulatory Aspects of Health Research*, Baltimore, MD: Johns Hopkins University Press.

Estraneo, A., Moretta, P., Loreto, V. et al. (2010). Late recovery after traumatic, anoxic, or hemorrhagic long-lasting vegetative state. *Neurology*, 75, 239–45.

Evans, M. (ed.) (1998) *Critical Reflection on Medical Ethics*, Standford, CT: Jai Press.

Fan, R. (2012). Confucian reflective equilibrium: why principlism is misleading for Chinese bioethical decision-making. *Asian Bioethics Review*, 4, 4–13.

Focarelli, C. (2009). Euthanasia. *Max Planck Encylocpedia of Public International Law* [Online]. Available at: http://www.mpepil.com/sample_article?id= /epil/entries/law-9780199231690-e793&recno=10& [Accessed 29 October 2011].

Freidson, E. (1988). *Profession of Medicine: A Study of the Sociology of Applied Knowledge*, London: University of Chicago Press.

Fromm, E. (1950). *Psychoanalysis and Religion*, New Haven, CT: Yale University Press.

Gawande, A. (2011). *The Checklist Manifesto: How to Get Things Right*, London: Profile Books.

Gibran, K. (1980). On children. *The Prophet,* London: Heinemann.

Gill, R. (2006). *Health Care and Christian Ethics*, Cambridge: Cambridge University Press.

Gilligan, C. (1982). *In a Different Voice: Psychological Theory and Women's Development*, Cambridge, MA: Harvard University Press.

Gomes, B. and Higginson, I. J. (2008). Where people die (1974–2030): past trends, future projections and implications for care. *Palliative Medicine,* 22, 33–41.

Griffin, J. (1997). *Value Judgement: Improving Our Ethical Beliefs*, Oxford: Clarendon Press.

Hallberg, I. (2004). Death and dying from old people's point of view. A literature review. *Aging Clinical and Experimental Research*, 16, 87–103.

Harris, J. (ed.) (2001). *Bioethics*, Oxford: Oxford University Press.

Harris, S. H. (1994). *Factories of Death: Japanese Biological Warfare, 1932–45, and the American Cover-up*, London; New York: Routledge.

Hart, J. T. (1971). The inverse care law. *The Lancet*, 297(7696), 405–12.

Have, H. t. and Gordijn, B. (2001). *Bioethics in a European Perspective*, Dordrecht: Kluwer Academic Publishers.

Hope, T., Savulescu, J. and Hendrick, J. (2008). *Medical Ethics and Law: The Core Curriculum*, Edinburgh, London: Churchill Livingstone Elsevier.

Illich, I. (1974). *Medical Nemesis*, London: Calder & Boyars.

Jones, J. H. (1993). *Bad Blood: The Tuskegee Syphilis Experiment*, New York: Maxwell Mcmillan International.

Jonsen, A. R. (2003). *The Birth of Bioethics*, New York; Oxford: Oxford University Press.

Lotze, M., Schertel, K., Birbaumer, N. et al. (2011). A long-term intensive behavioural treatment study in patients with persistent vegetative state or minimally conscious state. *Journal of Rehabilitation Medicine*, 43, 230–36.

Macklin, R. (2012). *Ethics in Global Health: Research, Policy and Practice*, Oxford: Oxford University Press.

Maslow, A. H. (1966). *The Psychology of Science: A Reconnaissance*, New York: Harper & Row.

May, W. F. (1975). Code, covenant, contract, or philanthropy. *The Hastings Center Report*, 5, 29–38.

Mellon, S., Northouse, L. L. and Weiss, L. K. (2006). A population-based study of the quality of life of cancer survivors and their family caregivers. *Cancer Nursing*, 29, 120–23.

Mepham, B. T. (2008). *Bioethics: An Introduction for the Biosciences*, Oxford: Oxford University Press.

Mill, J. S. (2004). *On Liberty*, Lanham, MD: Rowman & Littlefield Publishers.

Missler, M., Stroebe, M., Geurtsen, L. et al. (2011). Exploring death anxiety among elderly people: a literature review and empirical investigation. *Journal of Death and Dying*, 64, 357–79.

Mittleman, A. (2012). *A Short History of Jewish Ethics*, Chichester, UK; Malden, MA: Wiley-Blackwell.

Murray, T. H. (1996). *The Worth of a Child*, Berkeley: University of California Press.

Myser, C. (ed.) (2011). *Bioethics around the Globe*, New York: Oxford University Press.

Nagel, T. (1979). *Mortal Questions*, New York: Cambridge University Press.

Nie, J.-B., Tsuchiya, T. and Li, L. (2008). Japanese doctors' human experimentation in wartime China and its challenges for contemporary medical ethics. In: Baker, R. andMccullough, L. (eds) *The Cambridge World History of Medical Ethics*, New York: Cambridge University Press.

Noddings, N. (1984). *Caring: A Feminine Approach to Ethics and Moral Education*, Berkeley: University of California Press.

Nordenfeldt, L. (1987). *On the Nature of Health*, Dordrecht: Kluwer Academic Publishers.

Nussbaum, M. (2006). *Frontiers of Justice: Disability, Nationality, Species Membership*, London: The Belknap Press of Harvard University Press.

OECD. (2011). *Health at a Glance 2011: OECD Indicators*. OECD.

Office of History, NIoH. (1947). Nuremberg Code.

O'Neill, O. (2002). *Autonomy and Trust in Bioethics*, Cambridge: Cambridge University Press.

Papadopoulos, A., Vrettos, I., Kamposioras, K. et al. (2011). Impact of cancer patients' disease awareness on their family members' health-related quality of life: a cross-sectional survey. *Psycho-Oncology*, 20, 294–301.

Pappworth, M. H. (1967). *Human Guinea Pigs: Experimentation on Man*, London: Routledge and Kegan Paul.

Participants in the International Summit on Transplant Tourism and Organ Trafficking convened by The Transplantation Society and International Society of Nephrology in Istanbul, A. t. M. (2008). The Declaration of Istanbul on Organ Trafficking and Transplantation. The Declaration of Istanbul on Organ Trafficking and Transplantation [Online]. Available at: http://www.declarationofistanbul.org/index.php?option=com_content& view=article& id=82&Itemid=86 [Accessed 10 September 2012].

Popper, K. R. (1974). *The Open Society and Its Enemies*, London: Routledge & Kegan Paul.

Rawls, J. (1973). *A Theory of Justice*, London: Oxford Univerity Press

Roebuck, V. J. (2010). *The Dhammapada*, London: Penguin Books.

Royal Society of London (2012). *People and the Planet*, London: Royal Society.

Ryle, G. (1949). *The Concept of Mind*, London: Hutchinson

Sandel, M. (2012). *What Money Can't Buy: The Moral Limits of Markets*, London: Allen Lane.

Savulescu, J., ter Meulen, R. and Kahane, G. (eds) (2011). *Enhancing Human Capacities*, London: Wiley-Blackwell.

Scully, J. L., Baldwin-Ragavan, L. E. and Fitzpatrick, P. (2010). *Feminist Bioethics: At the Center, on the Margins*, Baltimore, MD: Johns Hopkins University Press.

Sen, A. (1999). *Development as Freedom*, Oxford: Oxford University Press.

—— (2009). *The Idea of Justice*, London: Penguin Books.

Singer, P. A. and Viens, A. M. (eds) (2008). *The Cambridge Textbook of Bioethics*, Cambridge: Cambridge University Press.

Snow, C. (2000). *The Search*, Cornwall: House of Stratus.

The Economist. (2007). A painful choice. *The Economist* [Online]. Available at: http://www.economist.com/node/8686503 [Accessed 17 August 2012].

Thomson, J. J. (1971). A defense of abortion. *Philosophy & Public Affairs*, 1, 47–66.

UC Atlas of Global Inequality. Health – global inequalities of health. Health – Global Inequalities of Health [Online]. Available at: http://ucatlas.ucsc.edu/ health.php [Accessed 10 September 2012].

United Kingdom. (2008). Human Fertilisation and Embryology Act 2008. United Kingdom: Parliament. Available at: http://www.legislation.gov.uk/ ukpga/2008/22/contents.

United Nations. (1948). The Universal Declaration of Human Rights. *Article 25*. [Online] Available at: http://www.un.org/en/documents/udhr/ index.shtml [Accessed 12 September 2012].

United Nations Educational Scientific and Cultural Organization. (2005). Universal Declaration on Bioethics and Human Rights. [Online] Available at: http://portal.unesco.org/en/ev.php-URL_ID=31058&URL_DO=DO_ TOPIC&URL_SECTION = 201.html [Accessed 12 September 2012].

United Nations Population Division. (2009). *World Population Prospects, the 2008 Revision*, New York: United Nations Population Division.

Ventatapuram, S. (2011). *Health Justice*, Cambridge, UK: Polity Press.

Waldby, C. and Mitchell, R. (2006). *Tissue Economies: Blood, Organs, and Cell Lines in Late Capitalism*, Durham, NC: Duke University Press.

Warburton, N. (2012). *Philosophy: The Basics*, London: Routledge.

WHO Department of Mental Health and Substance Abuse. (2011). *Mental Health Atlas 2011*, Geneva: World Health Organization.

World Health Organization. (1948). *Constitution of the World Health Organization*, Geneva: World Health Organization.

—— (2008). *Closing the Gap in a Generation: Health Equity through Action on the Social Determinants of Health: Commission on Social Determinants of Health Final Report*, Geneva: World Health Organization.

—— (2009). *Women and Health: Today's Evidence Tomorrow's Agenda*, Geneva: World Health Organization.

World Medical Association. (2008). World Medical Association Declaration of Helsinki – Ethical principles for medical research involving human subjects. *WMA General Assembly, 2008*. Seoul, Korea.

Yong, E. (2010). Dangerous DNA: the truth about the 'warrior gene'. *New Scientist*, 205(2755), 34.

INDEX